A Dissection Guide and Atlas to the Mink

David G. Smith
University of Richmond

Michael P. Schenk
University of Mississippi Medical Center

Morton Publishing Company
925 W. Kenyon Avenue, Unit 12
Englewood, Colorado 80110
http://www.morton-pub.com

Printed in the United States of America

10 9 8 7 6 5 4 3 2 1

ISBN: 0-89582-450-7

Preface

This dissection guide is designed to provide a comprehensive introduction to the anatomy of the mink for biology, zoology, nursing or pre-professional students undertaking a laboratory course in anatomy and physiology or basic vertebrate anatomy. The content and breadth of the material covered is primarily geared toward the university level, but may be appropriate for some advanced high school courses. The mink is an excellent organism for the study of vertebrate anatomy due to its similarities to humans and other mammals and it represents a viable, inexpensive alternative to the cat for teaching vertebrate anatomy. The relatively low cost and size of minks make them affordable and easy to store in the lab, and they are shipped already skinned — a feature that will save hours of tedious dissection time in lab. Another advantage of minks is that their use in labs does not deplete natural populations, since specimens are acquired from commercial mink ranches where they are raised for their fur.

In the past, few comprehensive sources dedicated to the anatomy of the mink have been available, causing many institutions to shy away from this animal as their specimen of choice for the study of vertebrate anatomy. This manual overcomes this pitfall by providing a convenient reference for vertebrate anatomy utilizing photographs, illustrations and descriptive text to thoroughly cover all major organs and organ systems of the mink at a level consistent with the curriculum of most comparative anatomy courses at the university level. To accommodate a wider range of laboratory approaches, the osteology of the cat is utilized as a comparative substitute (since mink skeletons are difficult to find) and sections focusing on the sheep heart and sheep brain are included. The concise design of this book allows it to serve as a supplement to other laboratory manuals that may be used in your course. Coverage of the organ systems follows a logical progression that maximizes the ease with which students can dissect relevant structures. The text is informative, highlighting material that can be applied to other life science courses. Chapters begin with lists of objectives to focus students' attention on the major concepts of each chapter. Full color photographs and illustrations provide accurate representations of the anatomy to facilitate identification of anatomical structures. Color micrographs of histological sections of relevant tissues accompany many of the photos and illustrations to give students an appreciation for the microanatomy associated with different tissues and organs. Tables are used throughout to conveniently summarize information presented in the text. Dissection instructions are set off from the text, while important terms are **boldfaced**. A glossary containing definitions of boldfaced terms is provided, along with a detailed index.

ACKNOWLEDGMENTS

Once again, we would like to show our appreciation to the many dedicated individuals who have played a role in the development and production of this manual. We have been extremely privileged to work with many of the same people on this project as on earlier endeavors. First and foremost we would like to thank Chris Rogers, Doug Morton and others at Morton Publishing for the opportunity to write this book. In sincere appreciation of their efforts and expertise, we would like to thank Kevin Kertz and Joanne Saliger for the handsome layout and design of this book. Darryl C. Smith, M.D., has again dedicated his time to painstakingly review the manuscript and provide valuable editorial comments and constructive criticisms. As always, Bill Armstrong provided excellent, detailed photography of the mink. Thanks to Robert Waltzer and Tim Schenk for providing bone specimens for use in the chapter detailing the skeletal system. Finally, we would like to kindly thank Dale Fishbeck for permission to use his photographs of the dissected eye.

Table of Contents

Introduction

This dissection guide is intended to provide an introduction to the anatomy of the mink for biology, zoology, nursing or pre-professional students undertaking a laboratory course in anatomy and physiology or basic vertebrate anatomy. The content and breadth of the material covered is primarily geared toward the university level, but may be appropriate for some advanced high school courses. The mink is an excellent "alternative" for a course in vertebrate anatomy due to its similarities to humans and other mammals. Additionally it is of a very manageable size, is relatively inexpensive (compared to cats) and is readily available. You will find that your specimens arrive "pre-skinned," a feature that will save hours of tedious dissection time in lab. Another advantage of the mink is that its use in labs does not deplete natural populations, since specimens are acquired from commercial mink ranches where they are raised for their fur.

Many features of this dissection guide allow the student quick access to the information presented and should facilitate use of this manual.

1. Each chapter begins with a list of objectives.
2. Color photographs and illustrations are provided for identification of anatomical structures.
3. Color micrographs of histological sections of relevant tissues accompany many of the photos and illustrations.
4. Tables are used throughout to conveniently summarize information presented in the text.
5. Dissection instructions are in a separate box, while important terms are **boldfaced**.
6. A glossary containing definitions of boldfaced terms is provided for quick reference.

Since, for some of you, this will be your first major dissection entailing many weeks of detailed observations, a review of proper dissection techniques and the terminology associated with the orientation of body planes and regions will serve as our starting point.

BASIC DISSECTION TECHNIQUES

1. **Practice safe hygiene when dissecting.** Wear appropriate protective clothing, gloves and eyewear, and DO NOT place your hands near your mouth or eyes while handling preserved specimens. While many of the preservatives currently used are non-toxic to the skin, they may cause minor skin or eye irritations in some individuals and should never be ingested. In general, the preservatives used on these specimens are desiccants and may dry out your skin after prolonged exposure. If fumes from your specimen irritate your eyes, ask your instructor about the availability of goggles.

2. **Read all italicized instructions CAREFULLY before making any incisions.** Make sure you understand the direction and depth of the cuts to be made — many important structures may be damaged by careless or imprecise cutting. For instance, while investigating the digestive system you do not want to damage structures in the circulatory system that you will need to identify later.

3. **Use scissors, a teasing needle and a blunt dissecting probe whenever possible.** Despite their popularity, scalpels usually do more harm than good and should not be relied upon as your primary dissection tool. Remember the purpose of "blunt" dissection is to separate muscles, organs and glands from one another without cutting them.

4. When instructed to "expose" or "view" an organ, you should attempt to remove all of the membranous tissues that typically cover these organs (fat, fascia, etc.). This may take 15–20 minutes in some cases, when done thoroughly. Your goal should be to expose the organ or structure as completely as possible. Many arteries and veins are embedded deeply in other tissues, while muscles are grouped closely together. These structures will require careful "cleaning" to adequately identify them.

5. A good strategy to use if working in pairs is to read aloud the directions from the book while your partner performs the dissection. These roles should be traded from section to section to give both of you a chance to participate. In addition to simply identifying the organs and structures from the photos and illustrations, make sure you read the descriptions of them in the text. You should be able to recognize each organ or structure *and* describe the function it performs in the body.

BODY PLANES AND REGIONS

Following the precedent set by the Editorial Committee of *Nomina Anatomica Veterinaria*, we have elected to use anatomical terminology that is most appropriate for quadrupedal animals such as the mink. As a result, some references to direction may differ from those commonly used to refer to corresponding regions on humans (e.g., the ventral surface of a quadruped is equivalent to the anterior surface of a human). The following terms will be used to refer to the regions of the body and the orientation of the organs and structures you will identify in the mink.

A section perpendicular to the long axis of the body separating the animal into cranial and caudal portions is called a **transverse** plane. The terms **cranial** and **caudal** refer to the head and tail regions, respectively. A longitudinal section separating the animal into right and left sides is called a **sagittal** plane. The sagittal plane running down the midline of the animal has a special name, the **median** plane. Structures that are closer to the median plane are referred to as **medial**. Structures further from the median plane are referred to as **lateral**. **Dorsal** refers to the side of the body nearest the backbone, while **ventral** refers to the side of the body nearest the belly. A longitudinal section dividing the animal into dorsal and ventral parts is called a **frontal** plane. **Proximal** refers to a point of reference nearer the median plane of the body than another structure (e.g., when your arm is extended, your elbow is proximal to your hand). **Distal** refers to a point of reference farther from the body's median plane than another structure (e.g., when your arm is extended, your elbow is distal to your shoulder). **Rostral** refers to a point closer to the tip of the nose.

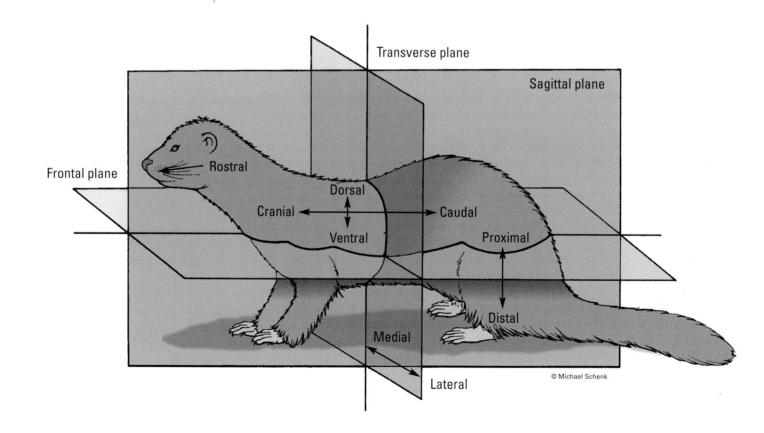

© Michael Schenk

External Features

CHAPTER 1

LABORATORY OBJECTIVES

After completing this chapter, you should be able to:

1. Identify the major external landmarks and features of the mink.

2. Identify the function of all indicated structures.

3. Determine the sex of your mink and the external structures unique to males and females.

GENERAL EXTERNAL FEATURES

INSTRUCTION

Obtain a mink from your instructor. Position your mink on its side in a dissecting pan so that you may observe the external features of your mink.

The mink (*Mustela vison*) has a long slender body, long bushy tail, short legs and sharp, powerful teeth. These characteristics allow minks to be extremely agile runners, excellent swimmers and efficient hunters. Minks den in small family groups along streams and lakes and their diet typically consists of small mammals, birds, eggs, frogs, crayfish and fish. Like most mammals, the body of the mink is divided into the **head**, **trunk** and **tail** regions (Figure 1.1). The trunk is further divided into the **thorax** and **abdomen** (which are separated internally by the diaphragm). The thorax houses the heart and lungs, while the abdominal region houses the major digestive, excretory and reproductive organs. Notice the sensory organs concentrated around the head. There are **eyes**, **ears** (pinnae), **nares** (used to sense chemicals dissolved in the air) and **vibrissae**. These organs all play a collective role in the mink's ability to sense and respond to stimuli in its environment. Minks are primarily nocturnal, venturing out under the cover of darkness in search of their prey. As a result, their eyes are adapted for excellent night vision and contain a specialized, reflective layer on the retina, the **tapetum lucidum**, which maximizes the amount of visible light that their photoreceptors can absorb. The tapetum lucidum is also responsible for the yellowish-green eyeshine that is characteristic of minks and other nocturnal mammals. The external coverings of the mink eye consist of upper and lower eyelids and a nictitating membrane that moves laterally from the medial corner of the eye. The vibrissae (commonly called whiskers) that are used for tactile sensations will most likely be missing on your specimen. The base of each vibrissa is attached to a sensory nerve, which is triggered by pressure or contact to the whisker. Other vibrissae are located over the eyes and on the cheeks and chin.

The minks used for dissection purposes are typically obtained from commercial mink ranches and sold for their fur; thus they are already skinned. They are usually also missing the distal portions of the forelimbs and hindlimbs, as these regions are removed during the skinning process. Another caveat concerning the mink is that commercial dealers keep most of the females for breeding purposes. As a result, you may find that the majority of specimens in your class are males. Because of the potential for reduced opportunity to view females, we have provided more photographs of females to compensate. Each front forelimb terminates in a **manus** (forefoot), and at the distal end of each hindlimb is a **pes** (hindfoot). Both forefeet and hindfeet are equipped with sharp **claws**, derived from keratinized epidermal tissue. Because of the orientation of the fore- and hindlimbs, minks (like humans) have a posture known as **plantigrade**, in which the heel and the digits of each foot rest on the ground. Cats and other mammals display a type of posture known as **digitigrade**, in which the heel of each foot is elevated above the ground. They are, essentially, walking or running on the tips of their "fingers" and "toes."

You should be able to determine the sex of your mink using external features. As a general rule, males are typically larger than females. While both sexes have many of the same structures, some of their locations differ in males and females. Both sexes have 8 **mammae** on the ventral surface of the abdomen. In females, these mammae are the external openings for the mammary glands, which store and secrete milk during lactation for the newborn young. The nipple of the "mammary gland" is actually an accumulation of small ducts leading from alveolar glands embedded in the adipose (fat) tissue of the thorax. Females usually give birth to 2–6 young at a time, although litter sizes of up to 10 are possible, and these young depend on milk secretions from the mother for nourishment until they are old enough to forage on their own. While males do possess mammae, they do not provide any known function. (NOTE: The mammae may be damaged or absent, and therefore difficult to locate, on your specimen due to the skinning process.) Both males and females possess an **anus**, located just ventral to the base of the tail (Figure 1.1). It is through the anus that undigested foodstuffs are eliminated (or egested) from the body. Typically, the term **excretion** is reserved for references to the elimination of metabolic waste products (e.g., nitrogenous wastes) from the body, while the term **egestion** applies to the elimination of indigestible material that the body cannot break down. A feature common to members of the Mustelidae is the presence of **anal sacs** (or glands). These structures produce a foul-smelling compound that gives weasels, ferrets, skunks, minks and otters their "characteristic" odor. (If you've ever kept a ferret as a pet, you know what I mean.) In fact, in many ferrets that are kept as pets, these glands are surgically removed to make the animals more esthetically appealing to their owners. In nature, however, these glands do serve an important purpose. Derived from modified apocrine glands, anal sacs discharge their products into the anal region, making the pheromones a component of the feces. These secretions are important in marking trails, establishing territories, courtship behavior, defense, and in recognizing individuals within a population.

FEMALE EXTERNAL FEATURES

Females have an external **vestibule** (or vaginal vestibule) ventral to the anus, near the base of the tail (Figure 1.1B). This region represents the opening to the reproductive pathway and serves as a channel for the release of excretory products (urine) from the body. The vestibule is the terminal portion of a long, tubular passage from the urogenital sinus in the mink, but it is a shallow depression in some mammals, including humans, that is flanked by lip-like folds of skin. These folds of skin are homologous to the labia in human females. A (very) small **clitoris** may be visible resting in a shallow depression along the mid-ventral line of the urogenital sinus. As a homologue to the male penis, this structure plays a similar role in sexual sensation and sends information about sexual stimulation to the brain. The entire region consisting of the labia, clitoris and vestibule are collectively referred to as the **vulva**.

MALE EXTERNAL FEATURES

In males, the **urogenital opening** is located at the distal end of the penis (Figure 1.1A). This represents the opening of the urethra which releases excretory products (urine) and semen in the adult. **Scrotal sacs** are present near the anus. (NOTE: one or both of the scrotal sacs and

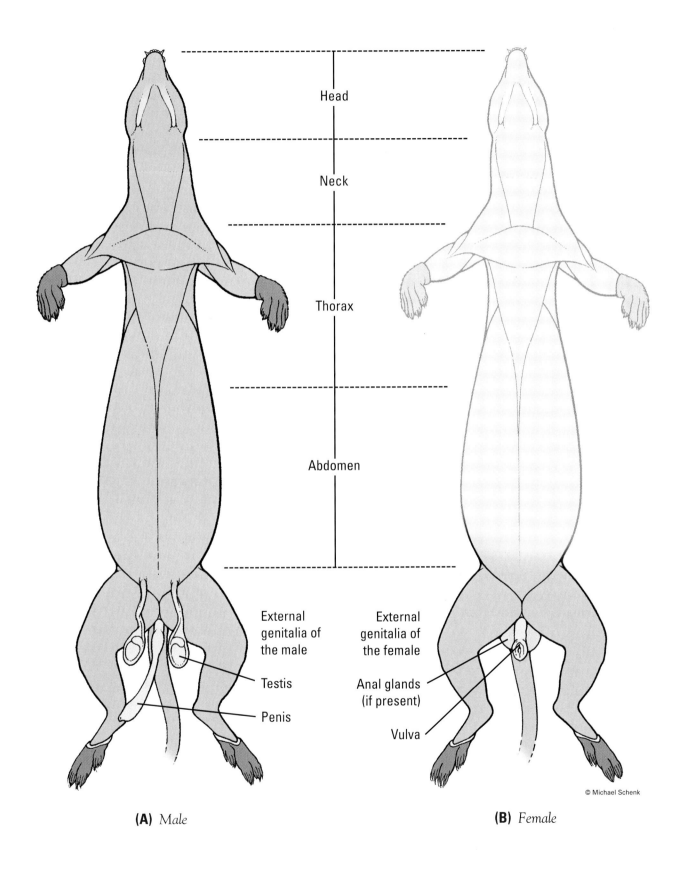

Head

Neck

Thorax

Abdomen

External genitalia of the male

Testis

Penis

External genitalia of the female

Anal glands (if present)

Vulva

© Michael Schenk

(A) *Male*

(B) *Female*

▲ **FIG. 1.1.** *Ventral view depicting external features of (A) male and (B) female mink.*

enclosed testes may be missing on your specimen due to the skinning process. If so, view another male mink with intact testes, or refer to the photographs to locate these structures.) During embryonic development, the testes, which originally form deep inside the abdominal cavity near the kidneys, migrate caudally and eventually descend into the scrotal sacs. Since sperm production is highly sensitive to temperature, the testes of most mammals are housed outside the body where temperatures are cooler than in the abdominal cavity. In humans, the temperature inside the testes is about 2°C cooler than the temperature within the abdominal cavity. If environmental temperatures drop too low, a special set of muscles known as **cremaster** muscles retracts the testes, pulling them closer to the body to conserve heat. In many mammals, the testes only descend during breeding seasons. A unique feature of the mink **penis** is the presence of an **os penis** (or **bacculum**). The **os penis** is an ossified structure that assists in maintaining an erection during copulation and allows the male to insert the penis fully into the long vaginal canal of the female. Humans lack such a bone. Another interesting feature of the penis in the mink is its size. The penis is quite long relative to the rest of the mink's body. This property enables the penis to fit completely through the tube-like vestibule and urogenital sinus of the female and deposit sperm directly at the bifurcation of the uterine horns — thus providing the sperm with a significantly shorter distance to swim to reach the eggs. Such "perfectly-matched" features have coevolved in concert through millions of years of natural selection operating on the individual variation in these traits that naturally exists in populations of animals.

Skeletal System

CHAPTER 2

LABORATORY OBJECTIVES

After completing this chapter, you should be able to:

1. Identify the different types of joints and discuss the movements they allow.

2. Identify the major features of the cat skull (as a substitute for the mink).

3. Identify the major elements of the axial and appendicular skeletal regions.

The skeletal system of vertebrates plays an important role in supporting the body and holding animals upright, yet it must allow for flexibility so that animals can perform a wide array of motions. Thus, while the skeletal system is composed of many individual calcified bones that are quite rigid, there are many different kinds of joints connecting these bones which permit movement. All mammals are members of the diverse Subphylum Vertebrata, which includes all animals with backbones. Minks belong to the Family Mustelidae, along with weasels, ferrets, wolverines, badgers, otters and skunks.

Mounted skeletons of minks are not likely to be as available, so we will provide a detailed analysis of the cat skeleton, since it is a popular option for teaching the osteology of a mammal comparable to humans. Since all mammals share a common ancestry, you will be able to see many bones in the cat that are homologous to both human and mink skeletons. **Homologous structures** are structures in different species that are similar due to shared common ancestry of the animals. This principle forms the basis for the field of comparative anatomy — a branch of zoology that uncovers the evolutionary relationships between related groups of animals by studying their anatomical similarities and differences. The mink and the cat are closely related animals and thus share many morphological similarities in their skeletal systems. They are both members of the Phylum Chordata, Subphylum Vertebrata, Class Mammalia and Order Carnivora, but belong to different families (cats are in the family Felidae, while minks are in the family Mustelidae). Humans also are members of the Phylum Chordata and Class Mammalia, but belong to the Order Primates. This nomenclature reflects the shared ancestry of these organisms, while at the same time illustrates the distinction between humans (and other primates) and carnivores. Thus we find the anatomy of the mink to be very similar to that of the cat. One significant difference in the osteology of the mink and the cat is that the os penis is absent in the cat but present in minks and many other mammals, especially rodents (Figure 2.1).

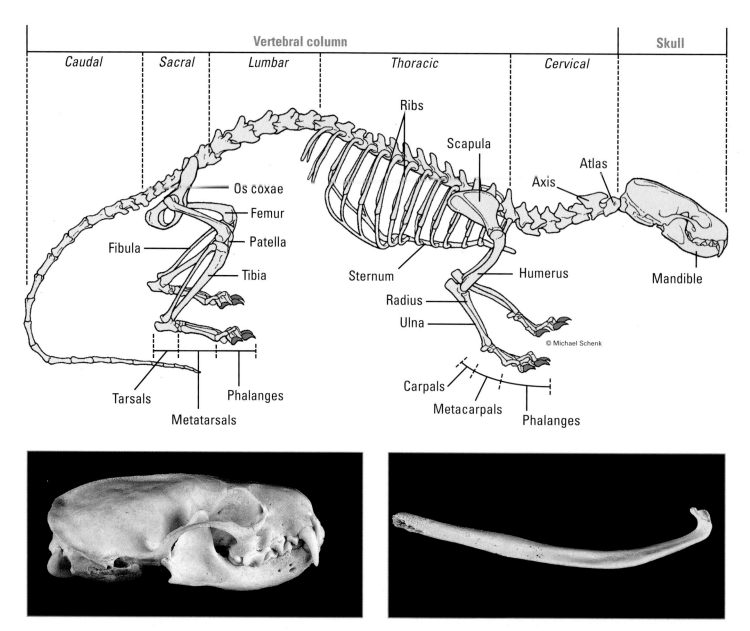

▲ **FIG. 2.1.** *Illustration of mink skeleton with photographs of skull and os penis.*

TYPES OF JOINTS

There are several different ways in which bones join together to form articulations. The type of joint present reflects both the kinds of movement that the particular joint will permit and the amount of strength the joint provides for support. In general, a joint can be classified into one of three basic groups. A **synarthrosis** is a joint in which there is little or no movement (e.g., sutures found between the bones of the skull or of the sacrum). These are by far the strongest joints, but at the expense of inhibiting movement. An **amphiarthrosis** is a joint that permits slight movement (e.g., gliding joints of the wrist), while a **diarthrosis** is a joint that permits very free movement between bones (e.g., spheroidal or condylar joints of the

shoulder or leg). Diarthroses are typically the weakest joints and subject to injury, but permit the widest range of motion of all three types of joints. The different classes of joints found in mammals are summarized in Table 2.1.

The skeleton is comprised of two different major regions: the axial skeleton and the appendicular skeleton. The **axial skeleton** consists of the skull, vertebral column and the rib cage. It forms the longitudinal axis of the body. The **appendicular skeleton** consists of the bones of the forelimbs and hindlimbs as well as the bones that attach the limbs to the axial skeleton, the pectoral and pelvic girdles (Figure 2.2).

TABLE 2.1. *Types of joints found in vertebrates and examples of where they occur in the body.*

JOINT	DESCRIPTION	EXAMPLE
Suture	Immovable connection between bones with interlocking projections; provides highest degree of strength but allows no motion	Cranial surfaces Sacrum
Hinge	Convex surface of one bone fits into concave surface of another; permits movement in only one plane	Metacarpals/Phalanges
Spheroidal (Ball-and-socket)	Round head fits into cup-shaped socket; permits greatest range of motion	Humerus/Scapula Femur/Ischium
Gliding	Flat or slightly curved surfaces oppose one another for sliding motion; permits only slight movement, but in all directions	Between Carpals Between Tarsals
Pivot	One bone turns around another bone as its pivot point; permits rotating movements	Radius/Ulna Atlas/Axis
Condylar	Two knuckle-shaped surfaces engage corresponding concave surfaces; permits movement in only one plane	Femur/Tibia

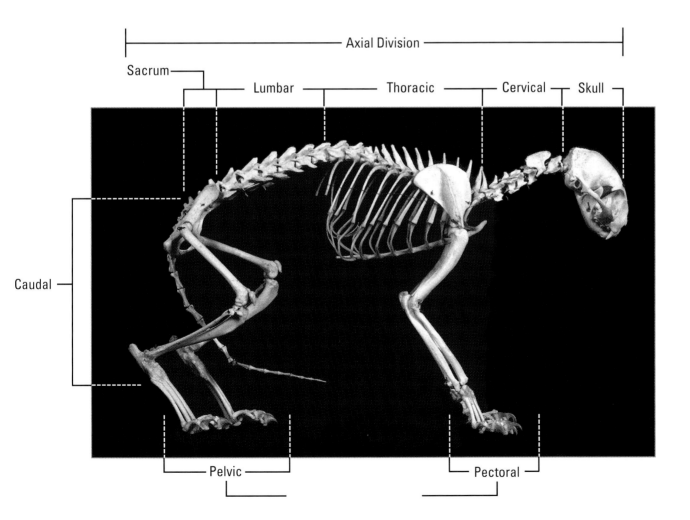

▲ **FIG. 2.2.** *Cat skeleton.*

AXIAL SKELETON

The Skull

The **skull** is actually comprised of several bones held together by immovable sutures (synarthroses) along the surfaces of the bones (Figures 2.3–2.4). As such, it forms a rigid, protective covering for the delicate brain and sense organs within. There are numerous **foramina** (singular = **foramen**) for the cranial nerves to exit the brain and innervate their respective organs, glands and muscles. The actual brain case is composed of several bones. The paired **frontal** bones form the roof of the brain case and the upper wall of the orbit. The **parietal** bones lie just behind the frontal bones. Together, the frontal and parietal bones constitute the majority of the dorsal portion of the brain case. A singular triangular bone, the **interparietal**, is located between the parietals and the occipitals and forms the caudal portion of the **sagittal crest** and the **lambdoidal ridge** which extends laterally along the back of the skull. The **temporal** bones form the ventro-lateral portion of the skull and contain several foramina (including the large external auditory meatus on each side). The **occipital** bone forms the back of the skull and contains the prominent **foramen magnum** which marks the end of the brain and the beginning of the spinal cord. The lateral side of the skull is supported by the **zygomatic** process which extends caudally from the orbit toward the base of the skull.

The anterior portion of the skull representing the nose and upper jaw is comprised of the **maxilla**, the **nasal** bones and the **premaxilla**. The most rostral bones in the upper jaw region are the paired premaxillae, which support the incisors. The maxilla supports the canines, premolars and molars. Cranial to these two bones are the paired nasal bones which cover the snout region. On the ventral surface of the upper jaw, locate the **palatine processes of the premaxillae** and the **palatine processes of the maxillae** (Figure 2.4B). These processes extend caudally to the **palatine** bones, which together constitute the hard secondary palate characteristic of mammals. Just caudal to the palatine bones and forming the upper roof of the nasal chamber are the **presphenoid** and the **basisphenoid**. Follow the basisphenoid caudally to the **basioccipital**. On either side of the basioccipital, locate the large **tympanic bulla** that houses the auditory organs of the cat.

The lower jaw in mammals is composed of a fused pair of single dentary bones called the **mandible** (Figure 2.5). This is one characteristic that separates mammals from all other classes of vertebrates (like fish, reptiles and birds). All of the teeth of the lower jaw are anchored in the mandible and many foramina are present for innervation of the teeth, lips

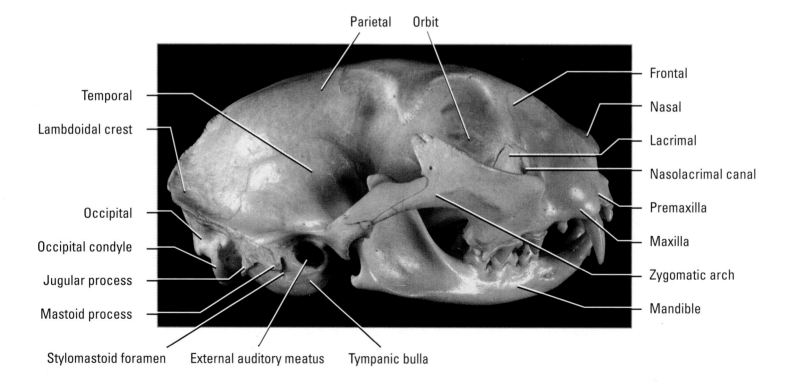

▲ **FIG. 2.3.** *Cat skull with mandible—lateral view.*

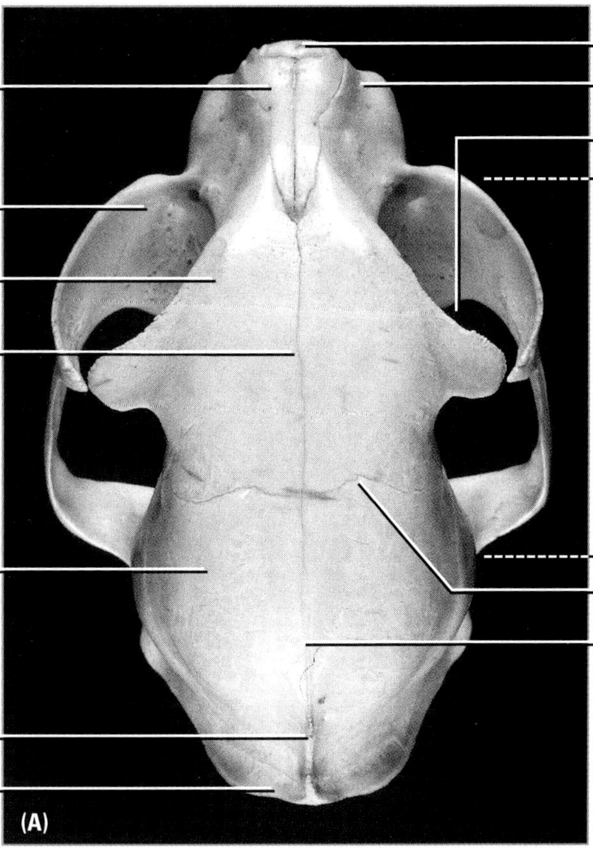

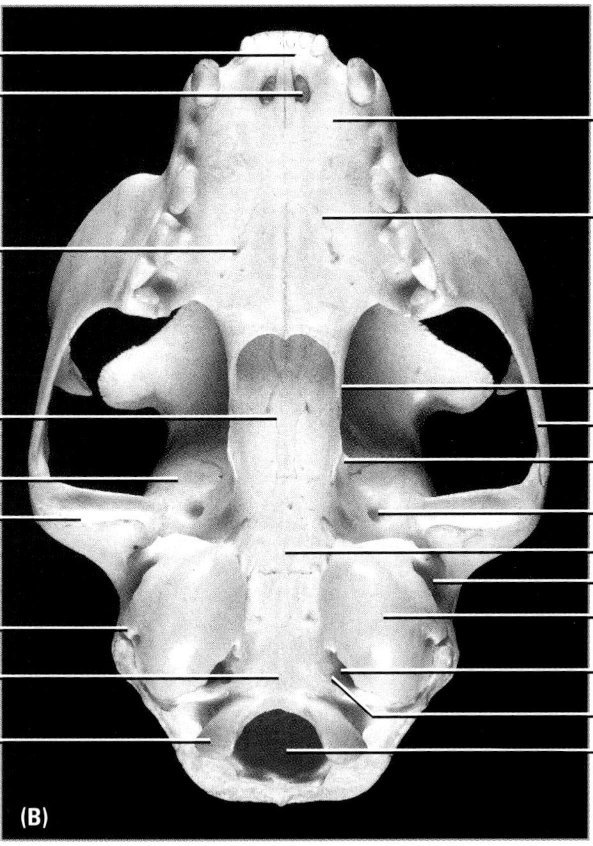

Nasal
Zygoma
Frontal
Frontal suture
Parietal
Sagittal crest
Lambdoidal ridge
(A)

Premaxilla
Maxilla
Eye orbit
Zygomatic arch
Coronal suture
Sagittal crest

Palatine process of premaxilla
Anterior palatine foramen
Posterior palatine foramen
Presphenoid
Alisphenoid
Mandibular fossa
Mastoid process
Basioccipital
Occipital condyle
(B)

Palatine process of maxilla
Palatine
Pterygoid process of palatine
Zygoma
Hamulus
Foramen ovale
Basisphenoid
Stylomastoid foramen
Tympanic bulla
Jugular foramen
Hypoglossal canal
Foramen magnum

▲ **FIG. 2.4.** Cat skull—dorsal view (A) and ventral view (B).

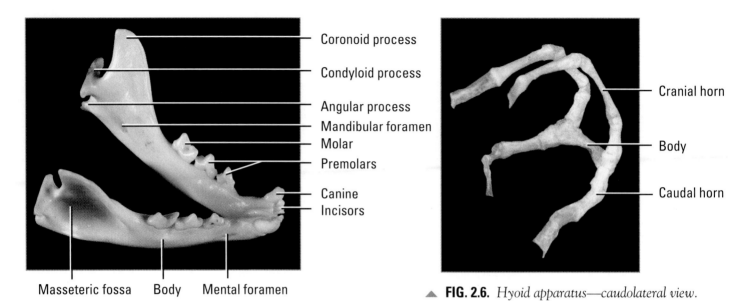

▲ **FIG. 2.5.** *Mandible—lateral view.*

▲ **FIG. 2.6.** *Hyoid apparatus—caudolateral view.*

and gums. The **coronoid process** is the site of insertion of the temporalis muscle. This large, powerful muscle gives carnivores their notoriously tenacious bite that, coupled with extremely sharp canines, premolars and molars, allows them to easily tear through flesh and bone. Notice the **condyloid process** of the mandible which forms the basis for the articulation between the mandible and the mandibular fossa of the zygomatic process. The bar-shaped design of this process is constructed to optimize a carnivore's ability to hold and subdue live, struggling prey, while minimizing lateral movement of the jaw. Omnivores, such as humans, have a more oval-shaped condyloid process which reflects an evolutionary adaptation to a more generalized diet.

A complex of bones associated with the neck region caudal to the mandible is the **hyoid bone** (Figure 2.6). This H-shaped bone consists of a **body** (the basihyal, forming the equivalent of a ladder rung) and **cranial** and **caudal horns**. Careful examination of the hyoid apparatus will reveal that it is actually composed of several smaller bones fused together. These bones are derived from the embryonic gill arches that are present in all mammals. In humans, the hyoid apparatus is greatly reduced. In cats, this complex serves as the origin of muscles for the tongue and larynx. In mammals, the hyoid apparatus plays an integral role in the feeding process, for its muscles participate in tongue movements, opening and closing the jaws and in swallowing.

Vertebral Column

To appreciate the subtleties of mammalian vertebrae, keep in mind that the vertebral column has two basic purposes: (1) to protect the delicate spinal cord that passes through it and (2) to permit flexibility, support and anchor points for muscle attachments. Thus all vertebrae have the same basic

morphology, with minor modifications depending on their specific location along the length of the spine. Vertebrae are comprised of a solid **centrum** on the ventral surface for structural support, the large central **vertebral canal** through which the spinal cord passes, **transverse processes** emanating from the lateral margins, a **spinous process** along the dorsal aspect (processes serve as anchor points for muscle attachment) and **articular facets** on the cranial and caudal aspect for articulations with neighboring vertebrae.

The 7 cervical vertebrae comprise the most cranial portion of the vertebral column. The skull joins the vertebral column at the first cervical vertebra, called the **atlas** (Figure 2.7). This is a highly specialized vertebra designed to fit precisely into the convex bulges in the base of the skull known as the **occipital condyles**. Uncharacteristically, the atlas lacks a centrum and spinous process. Instead it is primarily composed of two wing-like transverse processes. Notice that there are **transverse foramina** on either side of the vertebral canal near the transverse processes. The major arteries and veins that supply blood to the brain pass through these openings.

The second cervical vertebra is the **axis** (Figure 2.8). In contrast to the atlas, the axis has a prominent spinous process and an additional process (the **odontoid process**) projecting cranially from the rest of the centrum. The odontoid process is actually a fusion between the centrum of the atlas and the centrum of the axis that forms a pivot point for full rotation of the head. Small transverse processes are present along with transverse foramina. The remaining cervical vertebrae are very similar in morphology to one another and possess the characteristic features of vertebrae described earlier (Figure 2.9).

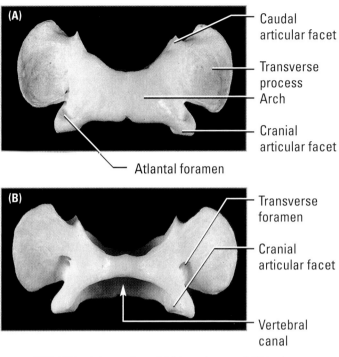

(A)

- Caudal articular facet
- Transverse process
- Arch
- Cranial articular facet
- Atlantal foramen

(B)

- Transverse foramen
- Cranial articular facet
- Vertebral canal

▲ **FIG. 2.7.** *Atlas—dorsal (A) and ventral (B) views.*

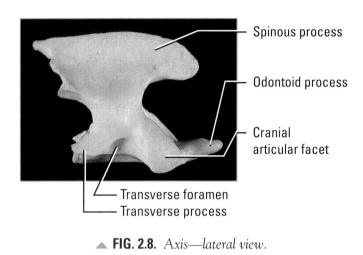

- Spinous process
- Odontoid process
- Cranial articular facet
- Transverse foramen
- Transverse process

▲ **FIG. 2.8.** *Axis—lateral view.*

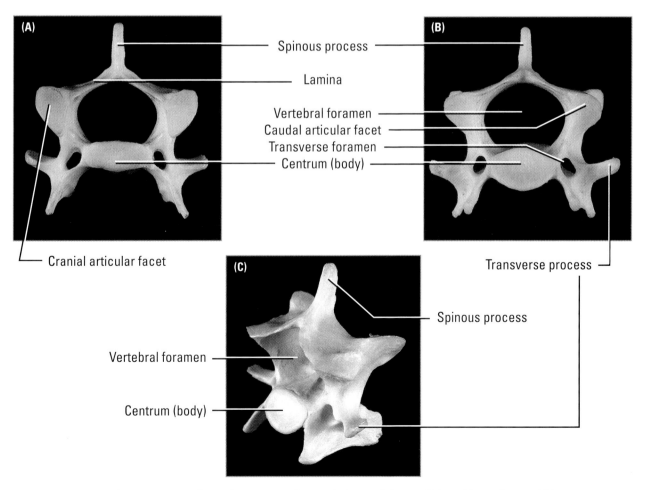

(A)

(B)

- Spinous process
- Lamina
- Vertebral foramen
- Caudal articular facet
- Transverse foramen
- Centrum (body)

- Cranial articular facet

- Transverse process

(C)

- Spinous process
- Vertebral foramen
- Centrum (body)

▲ **FIG. 2.9.** *Cervical vertebra—cranial view (A), caudal view (B) and lateral view (C).*

The thoracic region of the cat is composed of 13 **thoracic vertebrae** (14–15 in minks, 12 in humans) (Figure 2.10). On the articulated skeleton, notice the many **ribs** enclosing the chest region that extend from these vertebrae. These ribs provide protection and support for the heart and delicate lungs which lie inside the thoracic cavity. Each rib articulates on an **articular facet** of a thoracic vertebra. Other than this unique feature, thoracic vertebrae tend to be the least specialized of all mammalian vertebrae. They consist of a stout centrum, fairly short but prominent transverse processes, and a greatly elongated spinous process. The spinous processes of the first nine thoracic vertebrae project caudally in the cat, but the spinous processes of the last 4 thoracic vertebrae project cranially. In humans, all spinous processes point in the same direction (caudally).

Caudal to the thoracic vertebrae are the 7 **lumbar vertebrae** (5 in humans). These are the largest of the vertebrae and have no true ribs extending from them (Figure 2.11). They have relatively short spinous processes, but possess other prominent processes: **accessory processes**, **mamillary processes**, and **pleuropophyses**. These last processes represent the transverse processes of the vertebra with short, vestigial ribs fused to them.

A special group of 3 vertebrae fuse together during embryonic development in the cat (5 in humans) to form the **sacrum**, an especially strong region that supports the pelvic girdle and hindlimbs (Figure 2.12). Many of the characteristic features of vertebrae can be seen in "reduced form" in the sacrum. The pleuropophyses present in the lumbar vertebrae are now fused into a single structure in the sacrum.

Finally, the **caudal vertebrae** continue from the base of the sacrum to the tip of the tail (Figure 2.13). In minks, there are at least 18 caudal vertebrae, which become simpler in morphology as they progress caudally. Cranially, many of the caudal vertebrae possess characteristics typical of other vertebrae, but as they progress caudally, they begin to resemble small cylinders with concave openings. Human caudal vertebrae are less numerous, minimally functional and often fused. Collectively, they are referred to as the **coccyx** in humans. In mammals with long tails, the caudal vertebrae play an important role in locomotion, maneuverability and balance.

The **sternum** superficially resembles the vertebral column; it is composed of 8 segments (**sternebrae**) joined by cartilage with small cartilaginous projections (**costal cartilages**) which attach to the ribs (Figure 2.14). The most cranial segment of the sternum is the **manubrium**. The next six segments comprise the **body** of the sternum, while the final segment is the **xiphisternum** bearing a cartilaginous tip (the **xiphoid process**). In humans, the sternum is much flatter and contains only 7 costal cartilages, rather than the 8 seen in the cat's sternum.

Cats possess 13 pairs of **ribs** (humans have 12 pairs) which are all very similar in general morphology (Figure 2.15). The first 9 pairs are considered true ribs since they are always attached to the costal cartilage of the sternum. The distal ends of the last 4 pairs are not attached individually to the sternum. Rather, the first 3 pairs of these "false ribs" have costal cartilages attached to one another at their distal ends, which join to the sternum by a common cartilage at the location of the juncture of the ninth rib. The distal ends of the last pair of ribs float freely without sternal attachments. In general, a rib resembles a long, curved, flattened rod with an enlargement at its proximal end. This enlargement is the site of articulation with the vertebral column. This region is composed of the head (or **capitulum**) which articulates with the demifacets of two adjacent

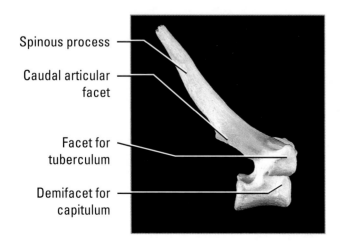

▲ **FIG. 2.10.** *Thoracic vertebra—lateral view.*

Spinous process
Caudal articular facet
Facet for tuberculum
Demifacet for capitulum

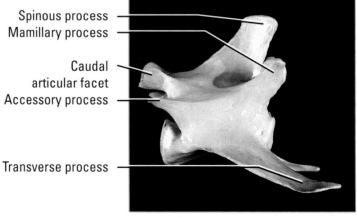

▲ **FIG. 2.11.** *Lumbar vertebra—lateral view.*

Spinous process
Mamillary process
Caudal articular facet
Accessory process
Transverse process

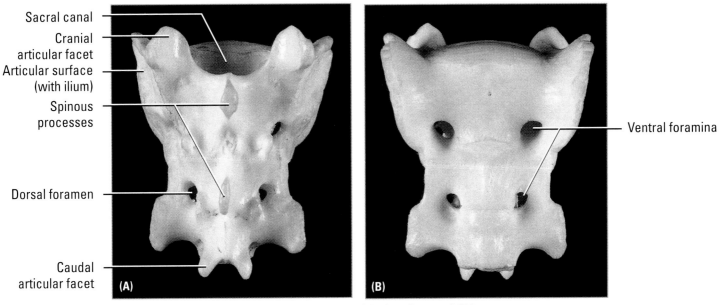

Sacral canal

Cranial
articular facet

Articular surface
(with ilium)

Spinous
processes

Dorsal foramen

Caudal
articular facet

(A)

(B)

Ventral foramina

▲ **FIG. 2.12.** *Sacrum—dorsal (A) and ventral (B) views.*

▲ **FIG. 2.13.** *Caudal vertebrae.*

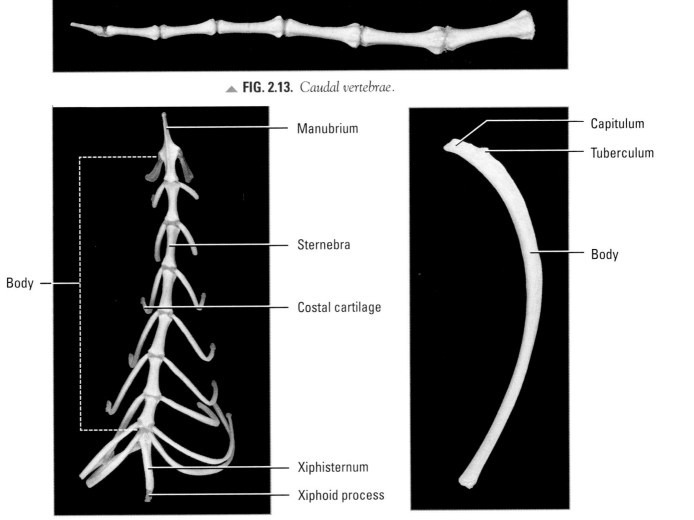

Manubrium

Sternebra

Body

Costal cartilage

Xiphisternum

Xiphoid process

Capitulum

Tuberculum

Body

▲ **FIG. 2.14.** *Sternum—ventral view.*

▲ **FIG. 2.15.** *Right rib.*

thoracic vertebrae and a **tuberculum** which articulates with the transverse process of one thoracic vertebra. Between the capitulum and tuberculum is a constricted portion known as the **neck**. Distal to the tuberculum is the **angular process**. The **body** (or shaft) of the rib has a pronounced **costal groove** running the length of the caudal surface. The position of this costal groove is useful in determining whether the rib you are examining is a right rib or left rib. If you are looking at the costal groove, then you are viewing the caudal surface of the rib. Also, the articulating surfaces of the capitulum and tuberculum are angled caudally (toward you, if you are looking at the side containing the costal groove).

APPENDICULAR SKELETON

Pectoral Girdle and Forelimbs

The **clavicle** in the cat is a curved, slender rod-shaped bone imbedded between the clavotrapezius and clavobrachialis muscles (Figure 2.16). In mammals with a body morphology adapted for running (e.g., cats, deer, dogs), the clavicle is greatly reduced or absent (e.g., horses) and has no true connections with neighboring bones. In humans, the clavicle is more prominent and articulates with the manubrium of the sternum and the acromion of the scapula.

The **scapula**, or shoulder blade, forms the base of the forelimb (Figure 2.17). This flattened, triangular bone is not actually attached to the axial skeleton; rather it floats in the glenoid cavity created by the muscle layers surrounding this region. These muscles hold the scapula tightly in place, but permit the flexible, fluid running motion characteristic of many mammals. The distal end of the scapula, however, is attached to the head of the humerus. The scapula is demarcated by three obvious borders: the **cranial border**, the **caudal border** (nearest the armpit) and the **dorsal border** (sometimes called the vertebral border since it is nearest the vertebral column). The lateral aspect of the scapula bears a prominent ridge known as the **tuberosity of the spine** (Figure 2.17A). This ridge separates the two lateral

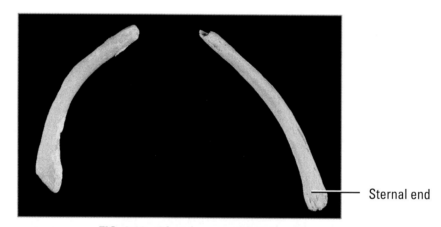

Sternal end

▲ **FIG. 2.16.** *Clavicle—cranial view.*

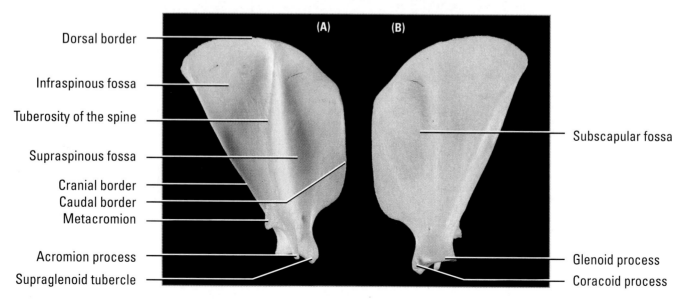

(A)   (B)

Dorsal border

Infraspinous fossa

Tuberosity of the spine

Supraspinous fossa

Cranial border

Caudal border

Metacromion

Acromion process

Supraglenoid tubercle

Subscapular fossa

Glenoid process

Coracoid process

▲ **FIG. 2.17.** *Scapula—lateral view (A) and medial view (B).*

surfaces (the **supraspinous fossa** and the **infraspinous fossa**) from one another. The **metacromion process** projects outward from the tuberosity of the spine near the **supraglenoid tubercle**. The medial surface of the scapula is known as the **subscapular fossa** (Figure 2.17B). The ventral end of the scapula terminates in the concave **glenoid fossa** which articulates with the head of the humerus.

The proximal portion of the forelimb is comprised of a single bone, the **humerus**. The head of the humerus articulates with the scapula and the distal end of the humerus articulates with the radius and ulna (Figure 2.18). The head of the humerus bears two processes: the **greater tuberosity** and the **lesser tuberosity**. Between these tubercles lies the **bicipital groove** through which a tendon of

the biceps brachii muscle travels. The shaft of the humerus bears two ridges which project distally from the head, the **pectoral ridge** and the **deltoid ridge**, which serve as insertion points for the pectoral muscles and deltoid muscles, respectively. The distal end of the humerus is comprised of two enlarged regions, the **medial epicondyle** and the **lateral epicondyle**. Nearby are the prominent **trochlea** and the less prominent **capitulum** with which the ulna and radius articulate, respectively.

The distal portion of the forelimb is comprised of two bones, the **radius** and **ulna** (Figure 2.19). The radius is the smaller of the two and articulates proximally with the humerus and distally with the ulna and a large carpal bone (the scapholunate). It is comprised of a proximal epiphysis (**head**) which is slightly concave to fit in the capitulum of the humerus, a long central shaft (diaphysis) bearing an

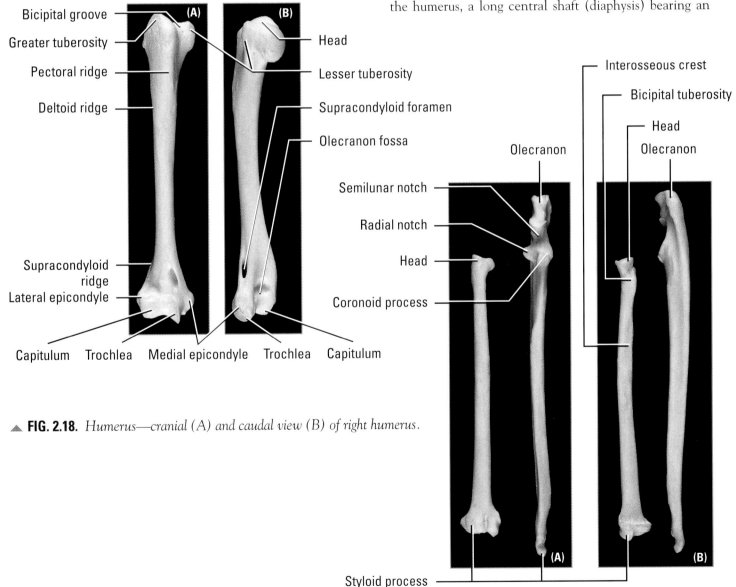

▲ **FIG. 2.18.** *Humerus—cranial (A) and caudal view (B) of right humerus.*

▲ **FIG. 2.19.** *Radius and ulna—cranial view (A) and caudal view (B).*

interosseous crest, and a distal epiphysis containing the **styloid process** which articulates with the wrist. The ulna contains the **olecranon** and a prominent **semilunar notch** which articulate with the humerus. There is a concave facet known as the **radial notch** just distal to the semilunar notch which serves as a point of articulation for the radius. An **interosseous crest** similar to that of the radius is found along the length of the ulna and the distal end terminates in the **styloid process** which articulates with the distal end of the radius and two carpal bones (the cuneiform and pisiform bones).

The 7 bones of the wrist are known as the **carpals**, while the 5 **metacarpals** and **phalanges** make up the forefoot (or manus) (Figure 2.20). In addition to the scapholunate, cuneiform and pisiform bones (mentioned previously), the trapezoid, hamate, capitate and trapezium bones comprise the remainder of the carpal bones in the wrist. These bones articulate with one another in gliding joints which permit only limited movement, but in all directions. The metacarpals articulate proximally with the carpals and distally with the phalanges and constitute the proximal end of the 5 digits common to many vertebrates. There are two phalanges in the thumb of the mink and three phalanges in each of the other four digits. A unique feature found in the cat that is not present in the mink (or in humans for that matter) is the presence of retractable claws on each distal phalanx. These claws are withdrawn into sheaths when not in use. Retractable claws represent a significant evolutionary adaptation of the feline family for capturing and grasping fast-moving, large prey.

Pelvic Girdle and Hindlimbs

Often referred to as the pelvis when paired together, each **os coxa** (or innominate bone) is a composite of the three major bones of the pelvic girdle, the **ilium**, the **ischium** and the **pubis** (Figure 2.21). The cranial portion of the os coxa is composed of the ilium. The ilium has an elongated **wing** which terminates in the dorsally located **crest of the ilium**. Nearer to the acetabulum is the **body of the ilium**. The **acetabulum** is a prominent cup-shaped indentation which articulates with the head of the femur. The caudal portion of the os coxa is comprised of the ischium and pubis. The **body of the ischium** projects caudally from the acetabulum. The **body of the pubis** is the most medial portion of the os coxa. The left and right os coxae fuse together along the **pubic symphysis** forming an extremely strong synarthrotic joint (or suture). Located at the cranial edge of the pubis is the **pubic tubercle**, a small, enlarged eminence representing the end of the pubis.

The **femur** is the long, proximal hindlimb bone (Figure 2.22). The **head** of the femur articulates with the acetabulum of the os coxa. The **greater trochanter** of the femur is

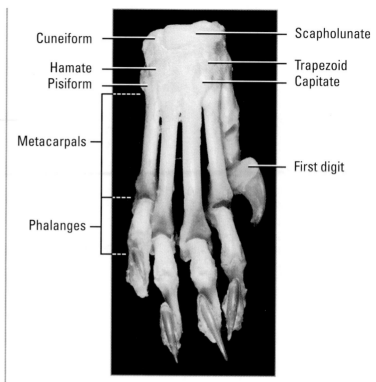

Cuneiform · Hamate · Pisiform · Metacarpals · Phalanges · Scapholunate · Trapezoid · Capitate · First digit

▲ **FIG. 2.20.** *Manus.*

the site for hip muscle attachments. The **lesser trochanter** of the femur lies just on the other side of the trochanteric fossa. The long, central shaft of the femur has an inconspicuous ridge, the **linea aspera**, along its length for muscle attachment to the femur. The distal portion of the femur is comprised of two condyles: the **medial condyle** and the **lateral condyle**, separated by the **intercondyloid fossa**. The smooth, rounded condyles articulate with the proximal end of the tibia. Notice that the knee region has a small bone, the **patella** (or "knee cap"), covering the juncture of the femur and the tibia and fibula (Figure 2.22C).

The **tibia** and **fibula** are the more distal hindlimb bones (Figure 2.23). The tibia is the larger of the two distal hindlimb bones. The proximal end of the tibia contains the concave **medial condyle** and **lateral condyle** which accommodate the respective convex condyles of the femur. Between the two tibial condyles is the **spine**. On the cranial aspect of the tibia three tuberosities can be identified: the **medial tuberosity**, the **tibial tuberosity** and the **lateral tuberosity**. The distal end of the tibia is defined by the **medial malleolus** which contains notches to accommodate tendons and contains concave facets which articulate with the tarsal bones. The fibula is a rather small, slender bone that has the **head** at its proximal end and the **lateral malleolus** at its distal end. The head of the fibula is fused to the lateral tuberosity of the tibia, but the lateral malleolus articulates with tarsal bones, much like the medial malleolus of the tibia.

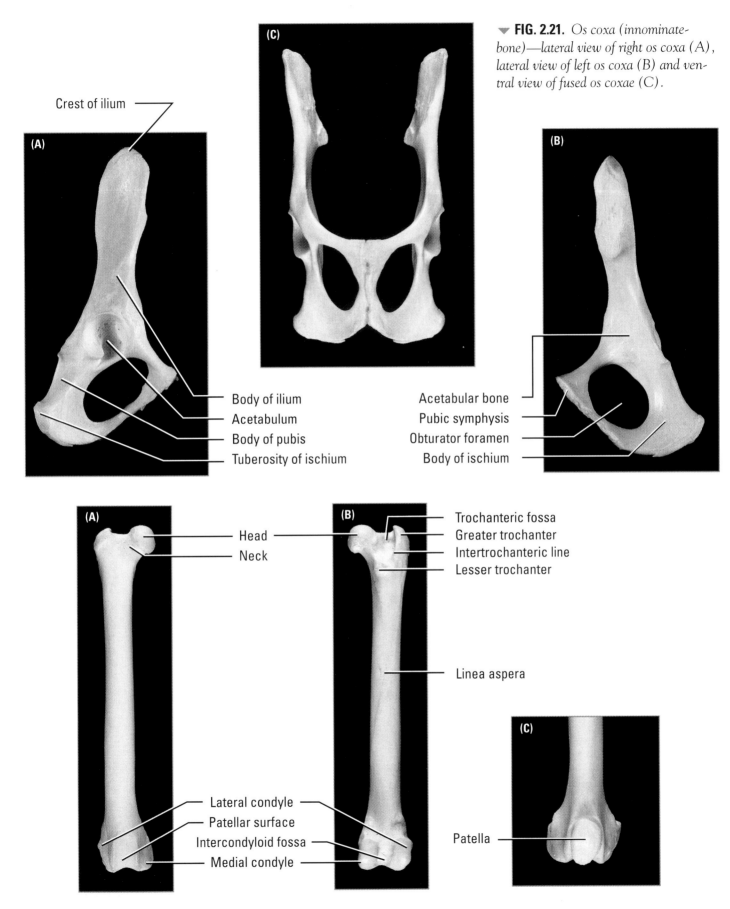

FIG. 2.21. *Os coxa (innominate-bone)—lateral view of right os coxa (A), lateral view of left os coxa (B) and ventral view of fused os coxae (C).*

Crest of ilium

(A)

(C)

(B)

Body of ilium
Acetabulum
Body of pubis
Tuberosity of ischium

Acetabular bone
Pubic symphysis
Obturator foramen
Body of ischium

(A)

(B)

Head
Neck

Trochanteric fossa
Greater trochanter
Intertrochanteric line
Lesser trochanter

Linea aspera

(C)

Patella

Lateral condyle
Patellar surface
Intercondyloid fossa
Medial condyle

FIG. 2.22. *Femur—cranial (A) and caudal views (B) of right femur with patella depicted on inset (C).*

The 7 "ankle" bones of the hindfoot, or pes, are collectively called the **tarsals**, and the remaining bones of the pes are the **metatarsals** and **phalanges** (Figure 2.24). The large bone in the hindfoot that forms the slight bulge in the back of the hindlimb in mammals is the **calcaneus** bone. This is homologous to our heel bone. The **talus** is the primary weight-bearing bone of the ankle and articulates with the tibia and fibula. The first digit in the hindfoot (corresponding to our big toe) is greatly reduced in most quadrupedal mammals. As a result, animals like the cat and mink have 4 primary phalanges. Cats display **digi-**tigrade locomotion, meaning they walk on the tips of their digits, or phalanges. Minks have a form of locomotion known as **plantigrade** locomotion, meaning they walk on the soles of their feet (their body weight is supported primarily by their metatarsals and tarsals as well as metacarpals and carpals, rather than their phalanges). This is similar to the type of locomotion that humans display.

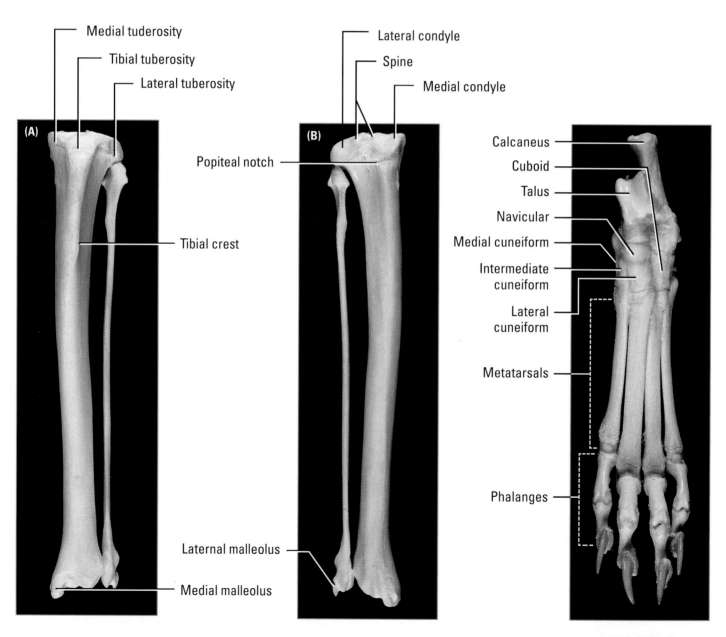

▲ **FIG. 2.23.** *Tibia and fibula—cranial (A) and caudal views (B) of right tibia and fibula.*

▲ **FIG. 2.24.** *Pes.*

Muscular System

CHAPTER

3

LABORATORY OBJECTIVES

After completing this chapter, you should be able to:

1. Recognize the microanatomy of different muscle tissues.

2. Identify the major superficial and deep muscles of the mink.

3. Identify the origins, insertions and actions of selected muscles in the mink.

4. Discuss the different types of movements that muscles perform.

FIG. 3.1. *Histology photographs of the three types of muscle tissue: (A) skeletal, (B) cardiac and (C) smooth.*

Muscles are designed with one basic purpose in mind — movement. Muscles work to either move an animal through its environment or move substances through an animal. In vertebrates, there are three basic types of muscle tissue — **skeletal muscle** and **cardiac muscle**, both of which possess striated fibers, and **smooth muscle**, sometimes called visceral muscle (Figure 3.1). Some of these muscles, like skeletal muscle, can be voluntarily controlled by the animal, while others, like cardiac and many smooth muscles, produce involuntary actions that are regulated by the autonomic nervous system. The muscles that you will dissect will be the skeletal muscles associated with the axial and appendicular portions of the skeleton.

The musculature of vertebrates is quite complex and requires patience and care to properly dissect each muscle away from its nearby structures. It is often difficult to tell where one muscle ends and another begins, which is compounded by the fact that many muscles occur in groups. You should pay careful attention to the direction of the muscle fibers. Often this will give you clues as to where two muscles cross or abut. Another aspect to note is the origin and insertion of each muscle. The **origin** is the less movable location on a bone where a muscle attaches, while the **insertion** is typically the more movable attachment. Sometimes muscles attach to tendons instead of attaching directly to bone. The direction a muscle exerts force also plays a role in its shape, where it inserts and originates (and sometimes its name). A muscle that **adducts** moves a limb toward the midline of the body. Conversely, a muscle that **abducts** moves a limb away from the midline of the body.

Remembering the unusual names of so many different muscles can be a daunting task. Keep in mind that in most cases the muscle's name bears out its origin and insertion, typically in that order. For instance the cricothyroid originates on the cricoid cartilage of the larynx and inserts on the thyroid

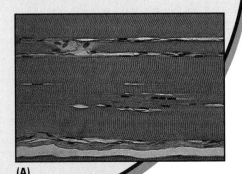

(A)

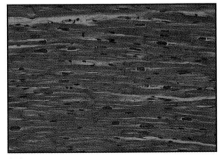

(B)

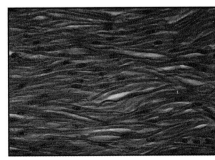

(C)

cartilage of the larynx. In many cases, other descriptors give an indication of the muscle's relative position to its neighbors (e.g., serratus dorsalis and serratus ventralis). Quite often these names still retain much of their original Latin terminology (e.g., gluteus maximus), and more than one acceptable name often exists for the same muscle (e.g., clavobrachialis = cleidobrachialis = clavodeltoid). We have tried to be consistent in our nomenclature of the muscles, but remember, there are many exceptions to these general "rules."

INSTRUCTION

Before you begin this section, you must first remove all of the fat and membranous fascia from the external surface of your mink. This process will take some time. The best strategy for removing this material is to use a blunt probe to tease the tissue away from the muscles. After all the extraneous tissue is removed and the superficial muscles have been exposed, lay your mink on its back to view the superficial ventral muscles of the head and neck.

THE HEAD AND NECK

Superficial Musculature

Examine the muscles of the ventral surface of the mink's neck (Figures 3.2–3.3 and Table 3.1). The largest and most cranial muscle of the ventral surface of the head is the **masseter**, the primary muscle involved in chewing. The masseter stretches from the zygomatic process of the skull to the masseteric fossa of the mandible. Ventral to the masseter (on the underside of the neck), locate the **mylohyoid**. This long, thin muscle runs longitudinally from the medial surface of the mandible to the basihyal (the body of the hyoid apparatus) where it meets the adjacent mylohyoid (from the other side of the body) at the midline of the body. The mylohyoid assists in raising the floor of the mouth. The **digastric** muscle is located along the medial side of the mylohyoid. It originates from the paraoccipital and mastoid processes of the skull and inserts on the ventral surface of the mandible. Its action is antagonistic to that of the masseter; the digastric depresses the mandible.

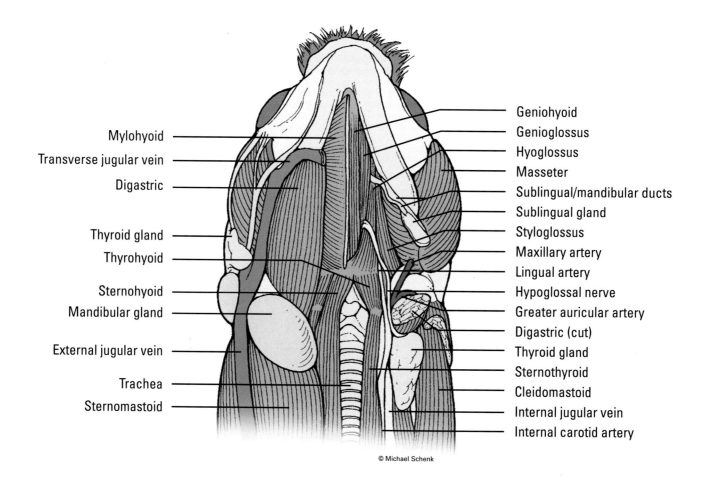

Mylohyoid
Transverse jugular vein
Digastric
Thyroid gland
Thyrohyoid
Sternohyoid
Mandibular gland
External jugular vein
Trachea
Sternomastoid

Geniohyoid
Genioglossus
Hyoglossus
Masseter
Sublingual/mandibular ducts
Sublingual gland
Styloglossus
Maxillary artery
Lingual artery
Hypoglossal nerve
Greater auricular artery
Digastric (cut)
Thyroid gland
Sternothyroid
Cleidomastoid
Internal jugular vein
Internal carotid artery

© Michael Schenk

▲ **FIG. 3.2.** *Superficial (mink's right) and deep muscles (mink's left) of the ventral aspect of the head and neck.*

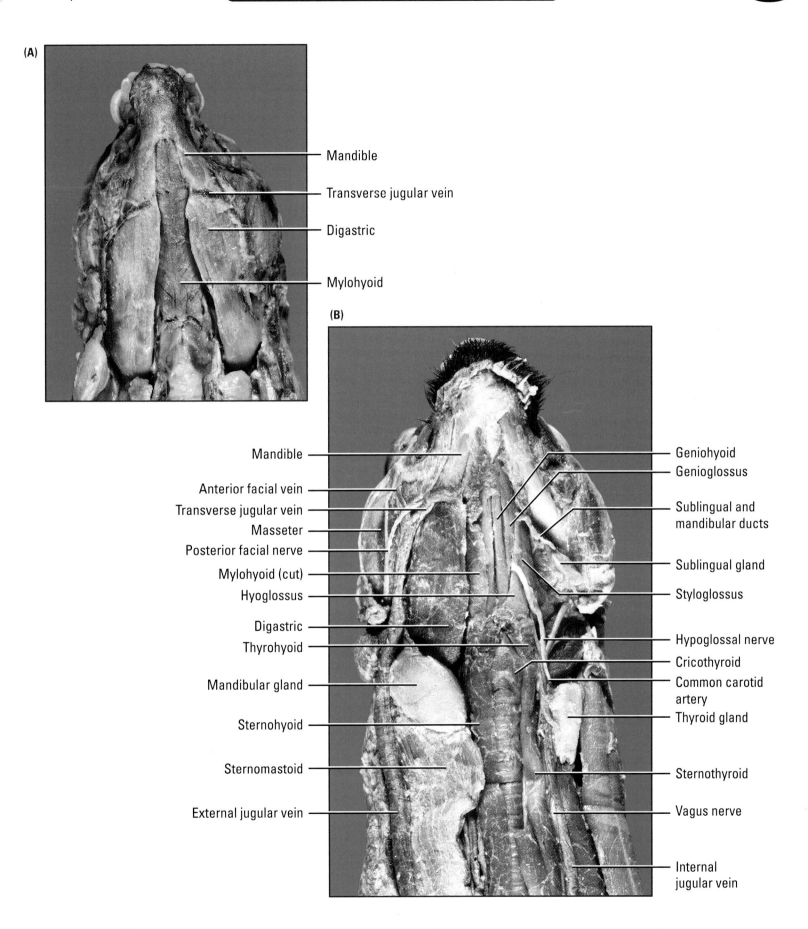

(A)

- Mandible
- Transverse jugular vein
- Digastric
- Mylohyoid

(B)

- Mandible
- Anterior facial vein
- Transverse jugular vein
- Masseter
- Posterior facial nerve
- Mylohyoid (cut)
- Hyoglossus
- Digastric
- Thyrohyoid
- Mandibular gland
- Sternohyoid
- Sternomastoid
- External jugular vein

- Geniohyoid
- Genioglossus
- Sublingual and mandibular ducts
- Sublingual gland
- Styloglossus
- Hypoglossal nerve
- Cricothyroid
- Common carotid artery
- Thyroid gland
- Sternothyroid
- Vagus nerve
- Internal jugular vein

▲ **FIG. 3.3.** *Superficial (mink's right) and deep muscles (mink's left) of the ventral aspect of the head and neck.*

TABLE 3.1. *Superficial muscles of the ventral aspect of the head and neck. Refer to Figures 3.2 and 3.3.*

MUSCLE NAME	ORIGIN	INSERTION	ACTION
Masseter	Zygomatic process	Masseteric fossa of mandible	Elevates mandible
Mylohyoid	Medial surface of mandible	Basihyal (meets adjacent muscle at midline)	Raises floor of mouth
Digastric	Paraoccipital process and mastoid process	Ventral surface of mandible	Depresses mandible

Deep Musculature

> **INSTRUCTION**
>
> *On the ventral surface of the neck use scissors (or a scalpel) to cut through the digastric and mylohyoid muscles on the left side of the animal to expose the underlying musculature.*

Identify the **geniohyoid** and **genioglossus** muscles lying directly underneath the mylohyoid that was cut (Figures 3.2–3.3 and Table 3.2). These two muscles originate from the mandibular symphysis and both assist in manipulating the tongue. The genioglossus actually inserts directly on the tongue, while the geniohyoid, as it name implies, inserts on the hyoid apparatus. Lateral to the genioglossus are the **hyoglossus** and **styloglossus**, two small muscles that also stretch between the hyoid apparatus and the tongue and manipulate the tongue. Further caudally, locate the **sternohyoid** which originates from the cartilage of the first rib and inserts on the basihyal, where it pulls the tongue backward. Medial to the sternohyoid is the **cricothyroid**. This small muscle originates on the cricoid cartilage of the larynx, inserts on the thyroid cartilage of the larynx and regulates tension of the vocal cords. Finally, identify the **thyrohyoid** which stretches from the thyroid cartilage of the larynx to the basihyal, and raises the larynx when it contracts.

TABLE 3.2. *Deep muscles of the ventral aspect of the head and neck. Refer to Figures 3.2 and 3.3.*

MUSCLE NAME	ORIGIN	INSERTION	ACTION
Genioglossus	Mandibular symphysis	Tongue	Manipulates tongue
Geniohyoid	Mandibular symphysis	Hyoid apparatus	Pulls tongue and hyoid forward
Hyoglossus	Lateral aspect of hyoid	Tongue	Manipulates tongue
Styloglossus	Hyoid apparatus	Tongue	Manipulates tongue
Sternohyoid	Cartilage of first rib	Basihyal	Pulls tongue backward
Cricothyroid	Cricoid cartilage	Thyroid cartilage	Regulates tension of vocal cords
Thyrohyoid	Thyroid cartilage of larynx	Basihyal (= body of hyoid apparatus)	Raises larynx

NECK AND PECTORAL REGION

Superficial Musculature

On the ventral side of the neck, locate the **sternomastoid**, a rather large muscle extending from the sternum cranially to its insertion point on the occiput of the skull (Figures 3.4–3.5 and Table 3.3). This muscle is primarily responsible for turning the head. Lateral to the sternomastoid, identify the **clavotrapezius** which extends from the occiput to the clavicle and the **clavobrachialis** which extends from the clavicle to the humerus. Together these muscles pull the humerus forward. Further caudally identify the **pectoralis major** and the **pectoralis minor**. These two large muscles work in concert to adduct the forelimb of the mink. They both originate on the sternum and insert on the proximal end of the humerus.

On the lateral surface of the mink's head, locate the prominent **temporalis** muscle running from the temporal fossa of the skull to the coronoid process of the mandible (Figure 3.6 and Table 3.4). This heavy muscle flexes the head and lifts the mandible. Caudal to the temporalis is the clavotrapezius (identified earlier) and caudal to the clavotrapezius is the **acromiotrapezius**. This is a large, broad muscle that originates along the spine and inserts on the scapula. Its role is to adduct and stabilize the scapula. Near the acromiotrapezius lie two smaller muscles: the **spinodeltoid** and the **spinotrapezius**. The spinotrapezius is another muscle inserting on the scapula, whereas the spinodeltoid inserts on the deltoid ridge of the humerus and abducts the

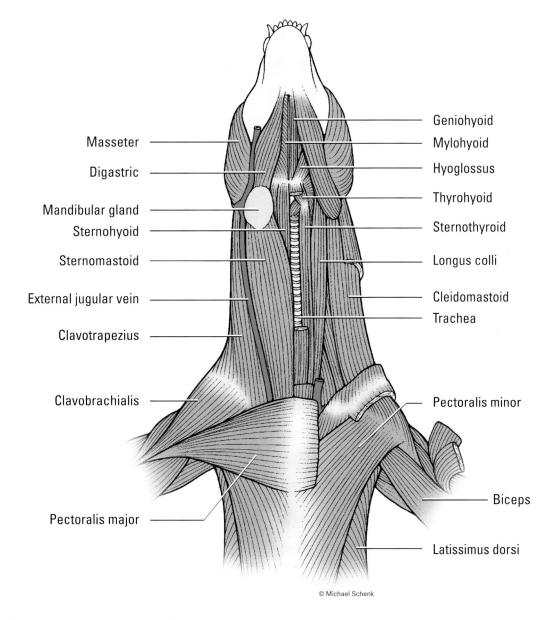

Masseter

Digastric

Mandibular gland

Sternohyoid

Sternomastoid

External jugular vein

Clavotrapezius

Clavobrachialis

Pectoralis major

Geniohyoid

Mylohyoid

Hyoglossus

Thyrohyoid

Sternothyroid

Longus colli

Cleidomastoid

Trachea

Pectoralis minor

Biceps

Latissimus dorsi

© Michael Schenk

▲ **FIG. 3.4.** *Illustration of superficial (mink's right) and deep muscles (mink's left) of the ventral aspect of the neck and pectoral region.*

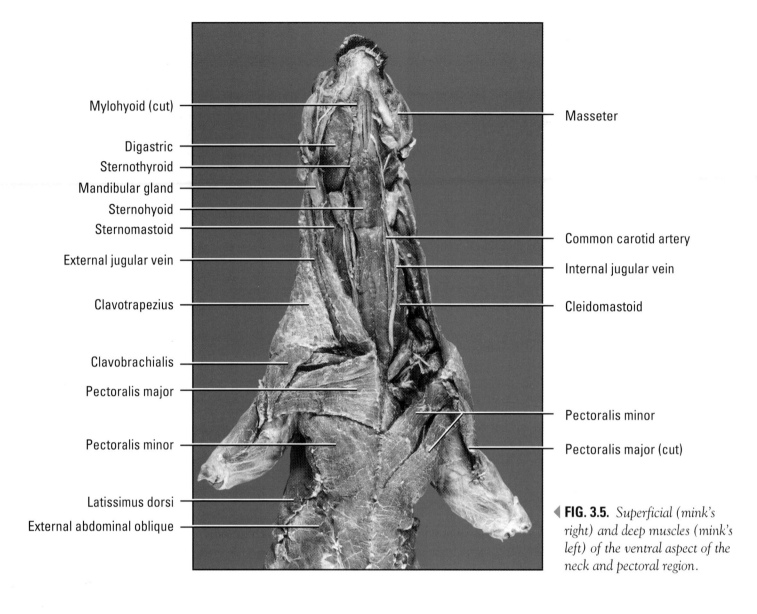

Mylohyoid (cut)

Digastric

Sternothyroid

Mandibular gland

Sternohyoid

Sternomastoid

External jugular vein

Clavotrapezius

Clavobrachialis

Pectoralis major

Pectoralis minor

Latissimus dorsi

External abdominal oblique

Masseter

Common carotid artery

Internal jugular vein

Cleidomastoid

Pectoralis minor

Pectoralis major (cut)

◀ **FIG. 3.5.** *Superficial (mink's right) and deep muscles (mink's left) of the ventral aspect of the neck and pectoral region.*

TABLE 3.3. *Superficial and deep muscles of the ventral aspect of the neck and pectoral region. Refer to Figures 3.4 and 3.5.*

MUSCLE NAME	ORIGIN	INSERTION	ACTION
Sternomastoid	Sternum	Occiput	Turns head
Clavotrapezius (Cleidocervicalis)	Occiput and dorsal midline of neck	Clavicle	Pulls humerus forward
Clavobrachialis (Cleidobrachialis)	Clavicle	Humerus	Pulls humerus forward
Pectoralis major	Sternum	Proximal humerus	Adducts forelimb
Pectoralis minor	Sternum	Proximal humerus	Adducts forelimb
Sternothyroid	Cartilage of first rib	Thyroid cartilage of larynx	Pulls larynx backward
Cleidomastoid	Clavicle	Occiput	Turns head

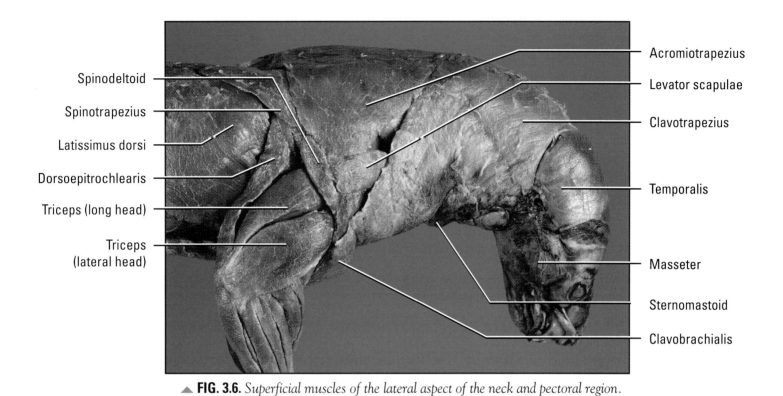

▲ **FIG. 3.6.** *Superficial muscles of the lateral aspect of the neck and pectoral region.*

TABLE 3.4. *Superficial muscles of the lateral aspect of the neck and pectoral region. Refer to Figure 3.6.*

MUSCLE NAME	ORIGIN	INSERTION	ACTION
Temporalis	Temporal fossa	Coronoid process of mandible	Flexes head, lifts mandible
Acromiotrapezius	Spine of axis to spinous process of 4th thoracic vertebra	Scapula	Adducts and stabilizes scapula
Spinodeltoid	Scapular spine	Deltoid ridge of humerus	Abducts humerus and pulls humerus forward
Spinotrapezius	Dorsal midline of thorax	Scapular spine	Rotates scapula backwards
Latissimus dorsi	Dorsal fascia of thorax	Medial surface of humerus	Pulls humerus backward
Dorsoepitrochlearis	Latissimus dorsi and teres major	Olecranon process of ulna	Extends forearm
Triceps, long head	Scapula	Olecranon process of ulna	Extends forearm
Triceps, lateral head	Lateral surface of humerus	Olecranon process of ulna	Extends forearm
Clavobrachialis	Clavicle	Medial surface of ulna	Flexes forearm

humerus. Another large, flat muscle, the **latissimus dorsi**, originates from the dorsal fascia of the thorax and inserts on the medial surface of the humerus. This broad muscle pulls the humerus backward. Caudal and ventral to the spinotrapezius is a small muscle that originates on the latissimus dorsi (and partially on the teres major). This is the **dorsoepitrochlearis**, one of the muscles that inserts on the olecranon process of the ulna and extends the forelimb. The triceps muscle (actually a complex of three muscles) is a major component of the proximal portion of the forelimb in the mink. The **triceps long head**, originating on the scapula, and the **triceps lateral head**, originating on the lateral surface of the humerus, both insert on the olecranon process of the ulna and assist in extending the forearm. The smaller and more cranial **clavobrachialis** originates on the scapula, inserts on the medial surface of the ulna and works antagonistically to flex the forearm.

> **INSTRUCTION**
>
> *On the ventral surface of the pectoral region use scissors (or a scalpel) to cut through the sternomastoid and pectoralis major muscles on the left side of the animal to expose the underlying musculature.*

One major muscle lies underneath the sternomastoid and pectoralis major. Locate the **cleidomastoid**, a long muscle running from the clavicle to the occiput (Figures 3.4–3.5 and Table 3.3). This is another muscle that turns the head of the mink.

Middle Musculature

> **INSTRUCTION**
>
> *To expose the middle layer of musculature on the mink, carefully cut through the clavotrapezius, latissimus dorsi and spinotrapezius and reflect these muscles.*

A large complex of muscles should be visible directly underneath the clavotrapezius (Figure 3.7 and Table 3.5). These are the **rhomboideus capitis, rhomboideus cervicis** and **rhomboideus thoracis** muscles. Collectively they originate on the spines of the first 4 thoracic vertebrae and insert on the vertebral border of the scapula. They adduct the scapula and pull it cranially. Ventral to the rhomboideus thoracis is the **atlantoscapularis**, a long muscle which runs diagonally alongside the rhomboideus capitis and then migrates dorsally along the rhomboideus thoracis to its insertion point on the scapula. The atlantoscapularis pulls the scapula forward. Next, locate the **levator scapulae** which runs longitudinally from the cervical vertebrae to the scapula. Its action is to depress the scapula. Finally, identify the **acromiodeltoid** stretching from the scapula to the humerus. This muscle pulls the humerus forward.

Deep Musculature

> **INSTRUCTION**
>
> *Cut through the rhomboideus capitis and reflect it back.*

FIG. 3.7. *Middle layer of musculature of the lateral aspect of the neck and pectoral region.*

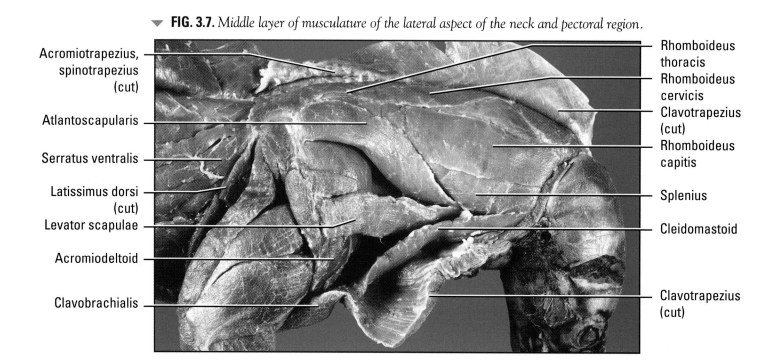

TABLE 3.5. *Middle muscles of the lateral aspect of the neck and pectoral region. Refer to Figure 3.7.*

MUSCLE NAME	ORIGIN	INSERTION	ACTION
Rhomboideus complex (R. cervicis, R. thoracis and R. capitis)	Spines of first 4 thoracic vertebrae	Vertebral border of scapula	Adducts scapula and pulls it cranially
Atlantoscapularis	Occiput	Dorsal edge of scapula	Pulls scapula forward
Levator scapulae	Transverse process of cervical vertebrae 3–7	Dorsal border of scapula	Depresses scapula
Acromiodeltoid	Acromion process of scapula	Deltoid ridge and tuberosity of humerus	Pulls humerus forward

Identify the large, broad **splenius** muscle underneath the rhomboideus capitis (Figure 3.8A and Table 3.6). This muscle originates from the spine of the first thoracic vertebra and inserts on the lambdoidal ridge of the skull. The splenius elevates the head.

INSTRUCTION

Cut through the splenius and reflect it back; then cut through the levator scapulae and atlantoscapularis and remove them. Finally remove the dorsoepitrochlearis, the triceps long head and the triceps medial head to completely reveal the underlying deep muscles of the pectoral region and forelimb.

Directly underneath the reflected splenius, locate the **semispinalis capitis** (Figure 3.8B and Table 3.6). This is a rather large muscle which extends from the last 4 cervical vertebrae and first 3 thoracic vertebrae to the lambdoidal crest of the skull and extends the neck when flexed. Ventral to this muscle, identify the **longissimus capitis**. This smaller muscle also extends from the spinous processes of the last 4 cervical vertebrae and assists in elevating the head. The **scalenus** is a small muscle embedded deep within the glenoid cavity of the forelimb, near the **rhomboideus profundus**. The scalenus pulls the ribs cranially, thereby assisting with the respiratory process of the mink. Further caudally, locate the **supraspinatus**, the primary shoulder muscle in this layer. The supraspinatus originates on the scapula and inserts on the greater tubercle of the humerus. Its primary action is to extend the shoulder. The **infraspinatus** is located just caudal to and alongside the supraspinatus. It originates from the scapula and inserts on the greater tubercle of the humerus where it assists in abducting and rotating the forearm. The smaller **teres major** is another muscle which originates from the scapula and controls the actions of the shoulder; however this muscle flexes the shoulder and adducts the forelimb. Next locate the **brachialis**. This minor muscle originates from the proximal margin of the humerus and inserts on the lateral surface of the ulna. Its primary role is to flex the forearm. Finally, identify the miniscule **anconeus** muscle, located near the "elbow." This muscle extends a short distance from the lateral epicondyle of the humerus to the olecranon process of the ulna and extends the forearm when flexed.

Deeper Musculature

INSTRUCTION

Reflect the forelimb dorsally to expose the muscles underneath the scapular region. Remove the semispinalis capitis, the longissimus capitis and the rhomboideus profundus.

Originating from the subscapular fossa, the **subscapularis** is a prominent muscle of the underside of the forelimb. It inserts on the lesser tubercle of the humerus and adducts and extends the shoulder (Figure 3.9 and Table 3.7). Also prominent is the **serratus ventralis**, a long, broad muscle that originates on the ribs, inserts on the dorsal edge of the scapula and aids in depressing the scapula. By reflecting the forelimb, you now have a full view of the scalenus muscle (actually a complex of 3 distinct muscles: the **scalenus anterior**, the **scalenus medius** and the **scalenus posterior**). The divisions between these three muscles are very indistinct, but careful preparation of the area should reveal their separations. The **longus colli** is another small muscle located just ventral to the scalenus complex. The longus colli bends the neck ventrally and laterally.

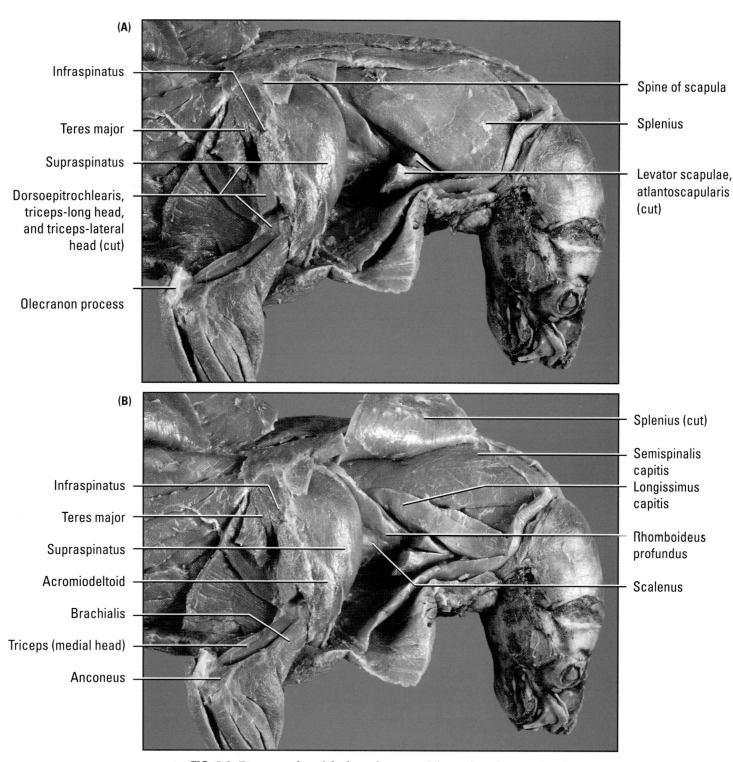

(A)

Infraspinatus

Teres major

Supraspinatus

Dorsoepitrochlearis, triceps-long head, and triceps-lateral head (cut)

Olecranon process

Spine of scapula

Splenius

Levator scapulae, atlantoscapularis (cut)

(B)

Infraspinatus

Teres major

Supraspinatus

Acromiodeltoid

Brachialis

Triceps (medial head)

Anconeus

Splenius (cut)

Semispinalis capitis

Longissimus capitis

Rhomboideus profundus

Scalenus

▲ **FIG. 3.8.** *Deep muscles of the lateral aspect of the neck and pectoral region.*

Deepest Musculature

The deepest muscles of the neck lie within the cavity created by removal of the semispinalis capitis and other muscles of that region (Figure 3.10 and Table 3.7). First locate the **rectus capitis posterior major** and the **obliquus capitis inferior**. Finally, find the **obliquus capitis superior**. These three muscles collectively control movements of the head and snout. They all originate from either the axis or atlas and insert on the skull (or atlas in the case of the obliquus capitis inferior).

TABLE 3.6. *Deep muscles of the lateral aspect of the neck and pectoral region. Refer to Figure 3.8.*

MUSCLE NAME	ORIGIN	INSERTION	ACTION
Splenius	Spine of first thoracic vertebra	Lambdoidal ridge of skull	Elevates head
Semispinalis capitis	Cervical vertebrae 3–7 and first 3 thoracic vertebrae	Lambdoidal crest of skull	Elevates the head
Longissimus capitis	Processes of last 4 cervical vertebrae	Cervical vertebrae	Extends neck
Scalenus	Transverse process of cervical vertebrae	Several anterior ribs	Pulls ribs cranially (assists in respiration)
Supraspinatus	Scapula	Greater tubercle of humerus	Extends shoulder
Infraspinatus	Infraspinous fossa of scapula	Greater tubercle of humerus	Abducts and rotates forearm
Teres major	Scapula	Medial edge of proximal portion of humerus	Flexes shoulder, adducts forelimb
Brachialis	Proximal margin of humerus	Lateral surface of ulna	Flexes forearm
Anconeus	Lateral epicondylar ridge of humerus	Olecranon process of ulna	Extends forearm

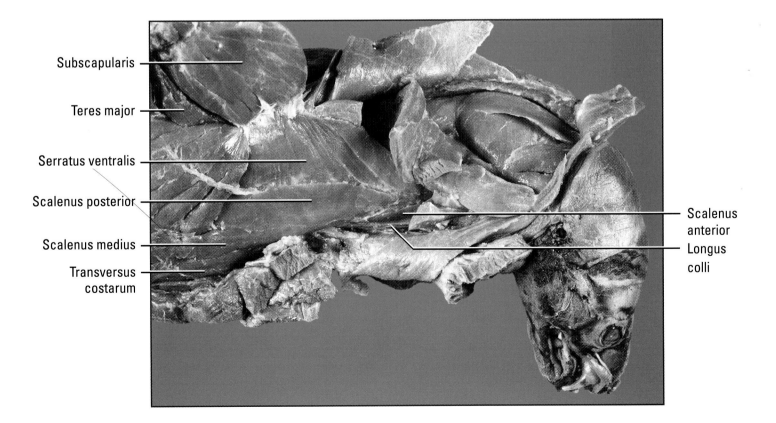

Subscapularis
Teres major
Serratus ventralis
Scalenus posterior
Scalenus medius
Transversus costarum

Scalenus anterior
Longus colli

▲ **FIG. 3.9.** *Deeper and deepest musculature of the lateral aspect of the neck and pectoral region.*

TABLE 3.7. *Deeper and deepest muscles of the lateral aspect of the neck and pectoral region. Refer to Figures 3.9 and 3.10.*

MUSCLE NAME	ORIGIN	INSERTION	ACTION
Subscapularis	Subscapular fossa	Lesser tubercle of humerus	Adducts and extends shoulder
Serratus ventralis	Ribs	Dorsal edge of scapula	Depresses scapula
Longus colli	First six thoracic vertebrae and transverse process of cervical vertebrae	Transverse process of 6th cervical vertebra and centra of cranial cervical vertebrae	Bends neck ventrally and laterally
Rectus capitis posterior major	Spinous process of axis	Lambdoidal crest of skull	Raises snout
Obliquus capitis inferior	Lateral surface of spine of axis	Transverse process of atlas	Rotates head
Obliquus capitis superior	Transverse process of atlas	Mastoid process of temporal bone	Flexes head laterally

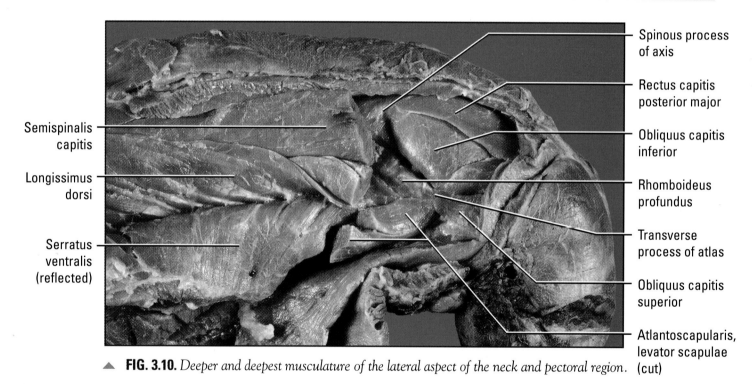

Labels: Spinous process of axis · Rectus capitis posterior major · Obliquus capitis inferior · Rhomboideus profundus · Transverse process of atlas · Obliquus capitis superior · Atlantoscapularis, levator scapulae (cut) · Semispinalis capitis · Longissimus dorsi · Serratus ventralis (reflected)

▲ **FIG. 3.10.** *Deeper and deepest musculature of the lateral aspect of the neck and pectoral region.*

FORELIMB

Lateral Superficial Musculature

Examine the lateral surface of the distal portion of the forelimb of your mink. Remember, due to the skinning process of these animals, the paws will be missing and some of the muscles in this region may have been damaged. Seven prominent flexors and extensors are visible on this side of the arm (Figure 3.11 and Table 3.8). Starting with the cranial aspect of the forelimb and moving caudally, first locate the **brachioradialis** muscle which lies along the cranial border of the humerus and inserts on the styloid process of the radius. This muscle supinates the paw. Next, identify the **extensor carpi radialis longus**, the **extensor digitorum communis**, the **extensor digitorum lateralis** and the **extensor carpi ulnaris**. These four muscles are responsible for actions that extend either the entire wrist or a few digits of the paw. The small **abductor pollicis longus** is visible at the most distal portion of the

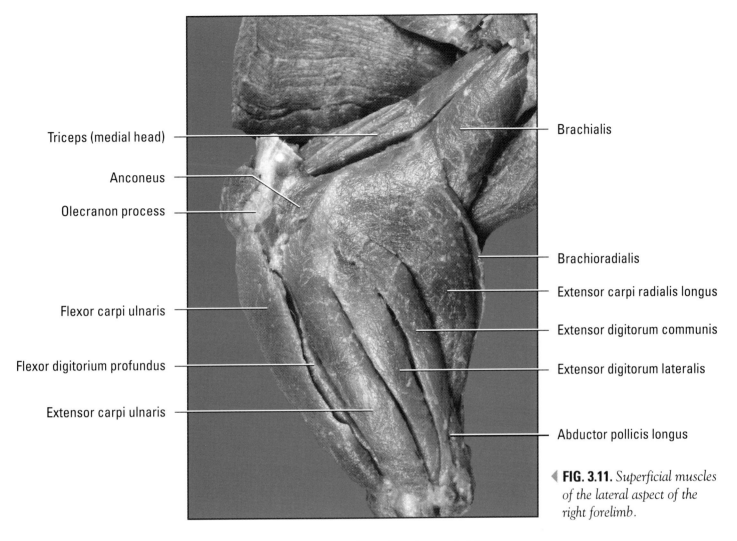

Triceps (medial head)

Anconeus

Olecranon process

Flexor carpi ulnaris

Flexor digitorium profundus

Extensor carpi ulnaris

Brachialis

Brachioradialis

Extensor carpi radialis longus

Extensor digitorum communis

Extensor digitorum lateralis

Abductor pollicis longus

◀ **FIG. 3.11.** *Superficial muscles of the lateral aspect of the right forelimb.*

TABLE 3.8. *Superficial muscles of the lateral aspect of the forelimb. Refer to Figure 3.11.*

MUSCLE NAME	ORIGIN	INSERTION	ACTION
Brachioradialis	Dorsal border of humerus	Styloid process of radius	Supinates paw
Extensor carpi radialis longus	Lateral epicondyle of humerus	2nd and 3rd metacarpals	Extends and flexes carpus (wrist)
Extensor digitorum communis	Lateral epicondyle of humerus below extensor carpi radialis	Phalanges of digits 2–5	Extends joints of digits 2–5
Extensor digitorum lateralis	Anterior face of lateral epicondyle of humerus	Digits 3–5	Extends 4th and 5th digits
Extensor carpi ulnaris	Lateral epicondyle of humerus	Tubercle of 5th metacarpal	Extends carpus, rotates wrist laterally
Abductor pollicis longus	Lateral surface of ulna and distal surface of radius	Radial side of 1st metacarpal	Extends and abducts pollex (thumb)
Flexor carpi ulnaris	Medial epicondyle of humerus and olecranon of ulna	Accessory carpal bone	Flexes carpus (wrist)

cranial border of the forearm. This muscle also extends the pollex (thumb). The most caudal muscle of the forelimb is the **flexor carpi ulnaris** which originates on the humerus and ulna and inserts on the accessory carpal bone. From here it flexes the wrist.

Medial Superficial Musculature

Now examine the medial surface of the distal forelimb. Again, starting from the cranial surface of the forearm, you will see the brachioradialis and the adjacent extensor carpi radialis longus (identified earlier). Adjacent to these muscles is the **extensor carpi radialis brevis**, a short muscle originating from the lateral epicondyle of the humerus and in-

serting on the 3rd metacarpal (Figure 3.12 and Table 3.9). This muscle extends the paw. The large **biceps brachii** is visible on the proximal portion of the forelimb, extending from the cranial edge of the glenoid cavity to the tuberosity of the radius. This muscle is the primary flexor of the forelimb. The smaller **pronator teres** is located near the insertion of the biceps brachii. As its name suggests, the pronator teres pronates the paw. Three major flexors of the wrist and digits can be found on the medial surface of the distal forelimb. Identify the **flexor digitorum profundus**, the **flexor carpi radialis** and the **flexor digitorum superficialis**. These muscles all originate on the humerus and insert onto the metacarpals or phalanges of the paw.

FIG. 3.12. *Superficial muscles of the medial aspect of the right forelimb.*

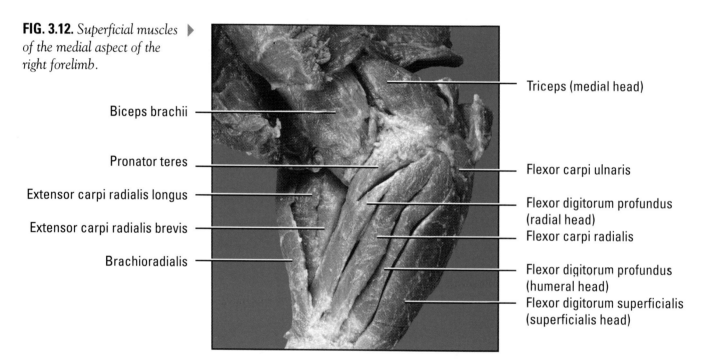

TABLE 3.9. *Superficial muscles of the medial aspect of the forelimb. Refer to Figure 3.12.*

MUSCLE NAME	ORIGIN	INSERTION	ACTION
Extensor carpi radialis brevis	Lateral epicondyle of humerus	3rd metacarpal	Extends paw
Biceps brachii	Cranial edge of glenoid cavity	Tuberosity of radius	Flexes forelimb
Pronator teres	Medial epicondyle of humerus	Medial border of radius	Pronates paw
Flexor digitorum profundus (radial head and humeral head)	Medial surface of ulna, medial epicondyle of humerus and medial surface of ulna shaft	Bases of distal phalanges	Flexes all digits
Flexor carpi radialis	Medial epicondyle of humerus	2nd and 3rd metacarpals	Flexes wrist
Flexor digitorum superficialis	Medial epicondyle of humerus and flexor digitorum profundus	Middle phalanx of digits 2–5	Flexes proximal and middle joints of digits 2–5

THE BACK

Superficial Musculature

Three major superficial muscles are present along the back of the mink. The most dorsal is the **serratus dorsalis**, which can be seen emanating from the spinous processes of the thoracic and lumbar vertebrae along the middorsal fascia. This long muscle inserts on the ribs and raises the ribs, thereby enlarging the thoracic cavity (Figure 3.13 and Table 3.10). Next identify the **serratus ventralis**. This muscle originates from the ribs and inserts on the dorsal edge of the scapula. When flexed, it depresses the scapula. Finally, locate the external abdominal oblique. Although technically an abdominal compressor, this muscle stretches along quite a large portion of the back and can easily be seen from this angle. The **external abdominal oblique** originates from the caudal ribs and the lumbodorsal fascia and inserts on the linea alba where in addition to compressing the abdomen it flexes the trunk.

Deep Musculature

Locate the **transversospinalis** underneath the original position of the serratus ventralis. This long, slender muscle stretches cranially from the transverse processes of the last few thoracic vertebrae to the transverse processes of the more cranial thoracic vertebrae (Figure 3.14). The muscle extends the vertebral column and is used to flex the vertebral column laterally. Next find the **iliocostalis**, located just ventral to the transversospinalis. The iliocostalis extends from the lateral surface of ribs to its insertion points three or four ribs cranially to the rib of origin. This muscle draws the ribs together when flexed. Finally locate the **longissimus dorsi**. This muscle lies underneath the original position of the serratus dorsalis. The longissimus dorsi originates from the neural spines of vertebrae and inserts on processes of more cranial vertebrae and extends the vertebral column.

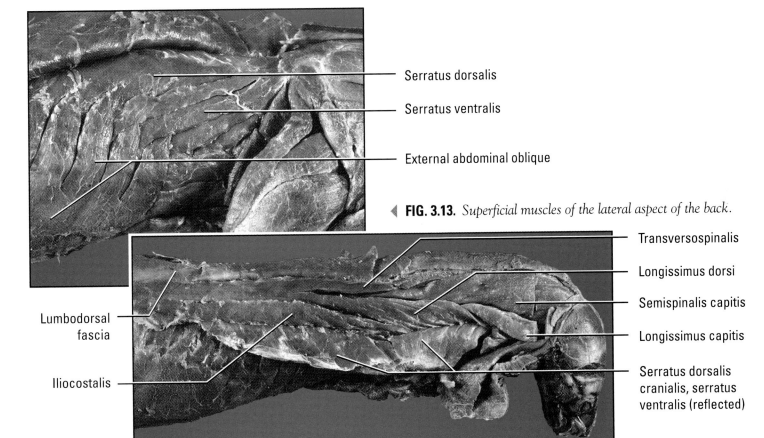

Serratus dorsalis

Serratus ventralis

External abdominal oblique

◀ **FIG. 3.13.** *Superficial muscles of the lateral aspect of the back.*

Transversospinalis

Longissimus dorsi

Semispinalis capitis

Longissimus capitis

Serratus dorsalis cranialis, serratus ventralis (reflected)

Lumbodorsal fascia

Iliocostalis

▲ **FIG. 3.14.** *Deep muscles of the lateral aspect of the back.*

TABLE 3.10. *Superficial and deep muscles of the back. Refer to Figures 3.13 and 3.14.*

MUSCLE NAME	ORIGIN	INSERTION	ACTION
Serratus dorsalis	Spinous processes of vertebrae	Outer surface of first nine ribs	Raises ribs, enlarges thoracic cavity
Serratus ventralis	Ribs	Dorsal edge of scapula	Depresses scapula
External abdominal oblique	Caudal ribs and lumbodorsal fascia	Linea alba	Compresses abdomen and flexes trunk
Transversospinalis	Transverse process of thoracic vertebrae	Transverse process of thoracic vertebrae farther cranially	Extends vertebral column and flexes laterally
Iliocostalis	Lateral surface of ribs	Lateral surface of 3rd or 4th rib cranial to rib of origin	Draws ribs together
Longissimus dorsi	Neural spines of vertebrae	Processes of more cranial vertebrae	Extends vertebral column

The Abdomen

The outermost abdominal muscle layer is comprised of the **external abdominal obliques** (identified earlier) which compress the abdomen and help flex the trunk (Figure 3.15 and Table 3.11). The muscle fibers of these muscles run diagonally across the abdomen at an oblique angle to the torso, and their name is derived from this arrangement. Underneath this layer you will find the **internal abdominal obliques**. Their muscle fibers run at a ninety degree angle to those of the external obliques. The innermost layer of abdominal muscles runs horizontally across the trunk (perpendicular to the long axis of the body) and is comprised of the **transversus abdominis** muscles. All three of these muscles insert on the linea alba, a long, thin, white band of connective tissue running down the midventral line of the abdomen, separating the ventral surface of the mink into left and right halves.

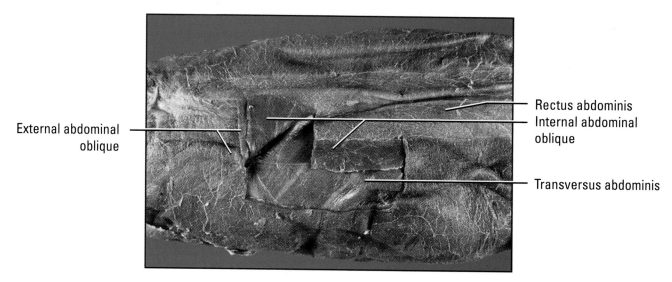

External abdominal oblique — Rectus abdominis — Internal abdominal oblique — Transversus abdominis

FIG. 3.15. *Abdominal muscles.*

TABLE 3.11. *Superficial and deep muscles of the abdominal region. Refer to Figure 3.15.*

MUSCLE NAME	ORIGIN	INSERTION	ACTION
External abdominal oblique	Caudal ribs and lumbodorsal fascia	Linea alba	Compresses abdomen and flexes trunk
Internal abdominal oblique	Lumbodorsal fascia and crural ligament between crest of ilium and pelvis	Linea alba	Compresses abdomen and flexes trunk
Transversus abdominis	Inner surface of caudal rib cartilage, transverse processes of lumbar vertebrae, ilium and crural ligament between ilium and pubis	Linea alba	Compresses abdomen and flexes trunk
Rectus abdominis	Pubic tubercle	1st and 2nd costal cartilages and sternum	Compresses abdomen

PELVIC REGION AND PROXIMAL HINDLIMB

Superficial Lateral Musculature

On the lateral side of the hindlimb there are six major muscles (Figure 3.16 and Table 3.12). The most cranial is the **sartorius**, which stretches from the ilium to the knee and extends the hindlimb and adducts the thigh. This muscle is actually more easily viewed from the medial surface of the hindlimb. The **tensor fascia lata** runs from the crest of the ilium and attaches to the front of the knee. Dorsal to the tensor fascia lata, locate the **gluteus maximus**, a rather large muscle originating on both the ilium and sacrum and inserting on the femur. This muscle abducts the thigh. Another prominent hindlimb muscle that also abducts the thigh (and flexes the hindlimb) is the **biceps femoris**. This is the largest muscle on the lateral side of the hindlimb and it stretches from the tuberosity of the ischium to the dorsal border of the tibia and patella. Caudal to the gluteus maximus is the **caudofemoralis** which abducts and extends the thigh. Finally, identify the **semitendinosus**, stretching along the caudal border of the hindlimb from the tuberosity of the ischium to the crest of the tibia.

Middle Lateral Musculature

INSTRUCTION

On the lateral side of the hindlimb, cut through the gluteus maximus, biceps femoris and tensor fasciae latae and remove these muscles to expose the next layer of musculature.

Three major muscles are visible in this middle layer (Figure 3.17 and Table 3.13). First identify the **gluteus medius**. This muscle originates from the lateral surface of the ilium, inserts on the greater trochanter of the femur and abducts the thigh. Next, locate the **vastus lateralis** originating on the greater trochanter of the femur and inserting on the vastus medialis and rectus femoris muscles. The vastus lateralis extends the hindlimb. Finally, identify the **tenuissimus**, a thin strip of muscle that extends from the base of the tail to the lateral surface of the hindlimb. This muscle flexes the hindlimb.

Deep Lateral Musculature

INSTRUCTION

Now cut and remove the tenuissimus, vastus lateralis, caudofemoralis and gluteus medius muscles.

Lying directly underneath the tenuissimus, locate the **semimembranosus** (Figure 3.18A and Table 3.14). You will only see a small portion of this muscle from the lateral side tucked underneath the large sciatic nerve running down the length of the hindlimb. The semimembranosus extends the hip and adducts the hindlimb. Near the semimembranosus is the **presemimembranosus**, a muscle which originates on the ischium, inserts on the femur and also extends the thigh. Next find the **gluteus minimus**, a small muscle that originates from the lateral surface of the ilium, inserts on the greater trochanter of the femur and abducts

TABLE 3.12. *Superficial muscles of the lateral aspect of the hindlimb. Refer to Figure 3.16.*

MUSCLE NAME	ORIGIN	INSERTION	ACTION
Sartorius	Ilium	Knee	Extends hindlimb, adducts thigh
Tensor fascia lata	Ilium and fascia of surrounding hip muscles	Fascia latae covering gluteus medius and vastus lateralis	Extends hindlimb
Gluteus maximus	Ilium and sacrum	Femur near greater trochanter	Abducts thigh
Biceps femoris	Tuberosity of ischium	Dorsal border of tibia and patella	Abducts thigh, flexes hindlimb
Caudofemoralis	Transverse processes of second and third caudal vertebrae	Lateral surface of femur near patella	Abducts and extends thigh
Semitendinosus	Tuberosity of ischium	Crest of tibia	Extends thigh and flexes hindlimb

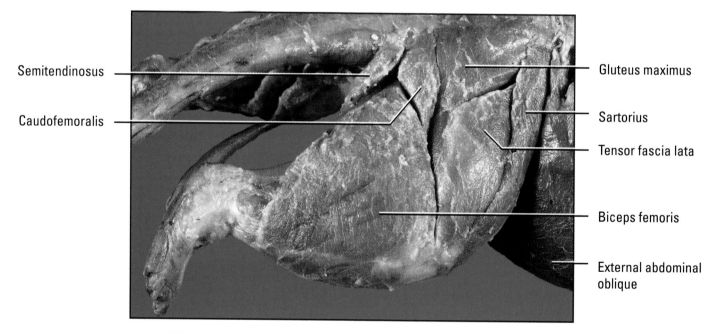

▲ **FIG. 3.16.** *Superficial muscles of the lateral aspect of the right hindlimb.*

TABLE 3.13. *Middle muscles of the lateral aspect of the hindlimb. Refer to Figure 3.17.*

MUSCLE NAME	ORIGIN	INSERTION	ACTION
Gluteus medius	Lateral surface of ilium	Greater trochanter of femur	Abducts thigh
Vastus lateralis	Greater trochanter of femur	Vastus medialis and rectus femoris	Extends hindlimb
Tenuissimus	Fascia covering base of tail	Lateral surface of hindlimb	Flexes hindlimb

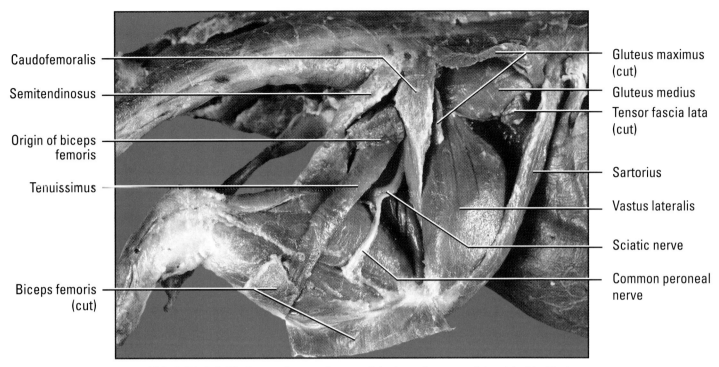

Caudofemoralis

Semitendinosus

Origin of biceps femoris

Tenuissimus

Biceps femoris (cut)

Gluteus maximus (cut)

Gluteus medius

Tensor fascia lata (cut)

Sartorius

Vastus lateralis

Sciatic nerve

Common peroneal nerve

▲ **FIG. 3.17.** *Middle layer of musculature of the lateral aspect of the right hindlimb.*

and rotates the thigh outward. The **rectus femoris** muscle should be evident near the cranial border of the thigh. This large muscle originates from the ilium, inserts on the crest of the tibia and extends the hindlimb. Another nearby extensor of the hindlimb is the **vastus intermedius** which extends from the cranial surface of the femur to the crest of the tibia as well. There are two major adductors of the thigh in this "deep" layer of muscle that insert on the femur: the **adductor magnus** and the **adductor brevis**. These two muscles may appear as one, but careful observation should reveal that they are actually separate muscles.

Now examine the proximal portion of the hindlimb carefully. Several more muscles should be visible in the "cavity" created by the removal of the caudofemoralis and tenuissimus (Figure 3.18B and Table 3.14). The four muscles in this region all rotate the thigh. The **gemellus inferior**, the **gemellus superior**, the **obturator internus** and the **quadratus femoris** all originate from the ischium and insert on the femur.

Superficial Medial Musculature

INSTRUCTION

Lay your mink on its dorsal side to gain access to the medial side of the thigh region. You may need to tie the hindlimbs "open" with string or pin them down to keep them apart while dissecting the muscles of this region.

On the medial side of the hindlimb, the most cranial thigh muscle is the **sartorius** which adducts the thigh and extends the hindlimb (Figures 3.19–3.20 and Table 3.15). The largest muscle on the medial side of the thigh is the **gracilis** which also adducts the thigh. Both muscles insert on the tibia and fascia of the knee, but the sartorius originates from the ilium, while the gracilis originates from the pubis and ischium.

Deep Medial Musculature

INSTRUCTION

On the left hindlimb of your mink, remove the sartorius and cut through the gracilis and reflect it back to expose the underlying deep musculature of the medial side of the hindlimb.

Identify the **rectus femoris**, a fairly prominent muscle stretching from the ilium to the tibial crest (Figure 3.20 and Table 3.15). The rectus femoris extends the hindlimb. Now locate the **adductor longus** and the **adductor femoris** muscles. These two muscles originate on the pubis and insert on the femur; they both adduct the thigh. The **semimembranosus**, identified earlier, is clearly visible from this aspect. Likewise, the **semitendinosus** is more visible from the medial aspect of the hindlimb. Both of these muscles extend the hip and flex the hindlimb.

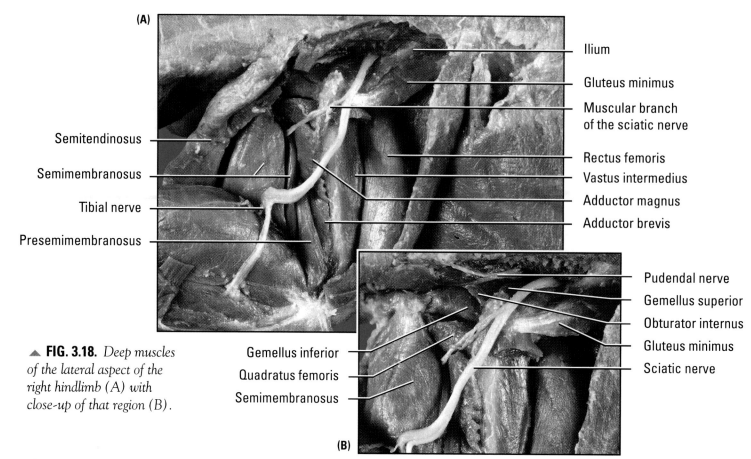

▲ FIG. 3.18. *Deep muscles of the lateral aspect of the right hindlimb (A) with close-up of that region (B).*

TABLE 3.14. *Deep muscles of the lateral aspect of the hindlimb. Refer to Figure 3.18.*

MUSCLE NAME	ORIGIN	INSERTION	ACTION
Semimembranosus	Tuberosity and ramus of ischium	Medial epicondyle of femur	Extends hip and adducts hindlimb
Presemimembranosus	Ischium	Femur	Extends thigh
Gluteus minimus	Lateral surface of ilium	Greater trochanter of femur	Abducts and rotates thigh outward
Rectus femoris	Ilium	Tibial crest	Extends hindlimb
Vastus intermedius	Cranial surface of femur	Tibial crest	Extends hindlimb
Adductor magnus	Ischium	Femur	Adducts thigh
Adductor brevis	Pubis	Femur	Adducts thigh
Gemellus inferior	Dorsal border of ischium	Trochanteric fossa of femur	Rotates thigh
Gemellus superior	Dorsal border of ischium	Trochanteric fossa of femur	Rotates thigh
Obturator internus	Inner surface of obturator foramen of os coxa	Trochanteric fossa of femur	Rotates thigh
Quadratus femoris	Ischial tuberosity	Greater trochanter of femur	Rotates thigh

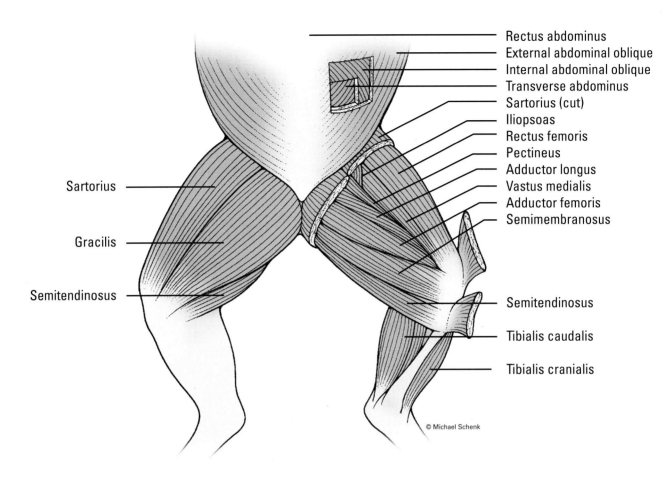

Rectus abdominus
External abdominal oblique
Internal abdominal oblique
Transverse abdominus
Sartorius (cut)
Iliopsoas
Rectus femoris
Pectineus
Adductor longus
Vastus medialis
Adductor femoris
Semimembranosus

Sartorius

Gracilis

Semitendinosus

Semitendinosus
Tibialis caudalis
Tibialis cranialis

© Michael Schenk

FIG. 3.19. *Ventral view of abdominal, pelvic and hindlimb musculature in the mink; superficial musculature depicted on mink's right, deep musculature depicted on mink's left.*

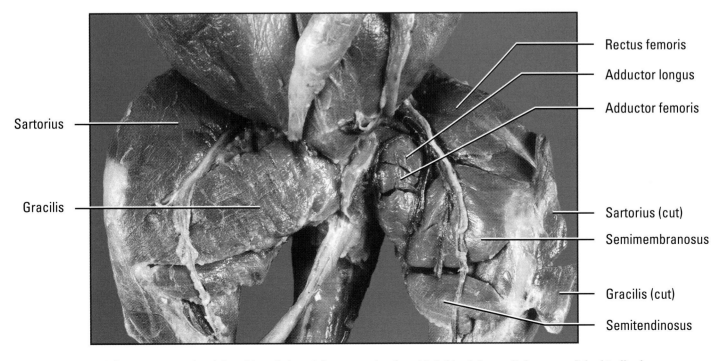

Rectus femoris
Adductor longus
Adductor femoris

Sartorius

Gracilis

Sartorius (cut)
Semimembranosus

Gracilis (cut)
Semitendinosus

FIG. 3.20. *Superficial (mink's right) and deep muscles (mink's left) of the medial aspect of the hindlimb.*

TABLE 3.15. *Superficial and deep muscles of the medial aspect of the hindlimb. Refer to Figures 3.19 and 3.20.*

MUSCLE NAME	ORIGIN	INSERTION	ACTION
Sartorius	Ilium	Patella, tibia and fascia of knee	Extends hindlimb, adducts thigh
Gracilis	Pubis and ischium	Medial surface of knee and hindlimb	Adducts thigh
Rectus femoris	Ilium	Tibial crest	Extends hindlimb
Adductor longus	Pubis	Femur	Adducts thigh
Adductor femoris	Ramus of pubis and ischium	Shaft of femur	Adducts thigh
Semimembranosus	Ischium	Medial surface of knee and hindlimb	Extends thigh and flexes hindlimb
Semitendinosus	Fascia covering base of tail	Medial surface of hindlimb	Extends thigh and flexes hindlimb

Deeper Medial Musculature

Now examine the proximal portion of the medial side of the hindlimb more closely. Close inspection of this region should reveal several other smaller muscles lying between the rectus femoris and the adductor longus and adductor femoris (Figure 3.21 and Table 3.16). The **vastus medialis** extends from the shaft of the femur distally to the patella and the head of the tibia where it inserts and assists in extending the hindlimb. Closer to the hip joint, locate the small **iliopsoas** and **pectineus** muscles. These minor muscles flex the hip and adduct the thigh.

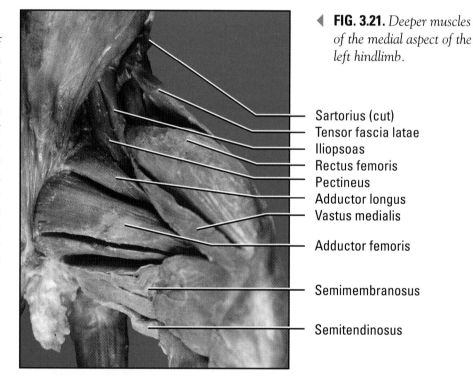

◀ **FIG. 3.21.** *Deeper muscles of the medial aspect of the left hindlimb.*

Sartorius (cut)
Tensor fascia latae
Iliopsoas
Rectus femoris
Pectineus
Adductor longus
Vastus medialis

Adductor femoris

Semimembranosus

Semitendinosus

TABLE 3.16. *Deeper muscles of the medial aspect of the hindlimb. Refer to Figure 3.21.*

MUSCLE NAME	ORIGIN	INSERTION	ACTION
Vastus medialis	Shaft of femur	Patella and head of tibia	Extends hindlimb
Iliopsoas	Last few thoracic vertebrae and all lumbar vertebrae	Lesser trochanter of femur	Flexes thigh
Pectineus	Cranial edge of pubis	Proximal shaft of femur	Flexes hip and adducts thigh

DISTAL HINDLIMB

Superficial Lateral Musculature

Examine the lateral aspect of the distal portion of the right hindlimb of your mink (Figure 3.22 and Table 3.17). The most cranial muscle in this region is the **tibialis cranialis**, so named because it extends along the cranial surface of the tibia to its insertion point on the first metatarsal. Its role is to flex the hindfoot. Running adjacent to the tibialis cranialis is the **extensor digitorum longus**, a shorter muscle that becomes noticeable only along the most distal portion of the hindlimb. It originates underneath the tibialis cranialis on the lateral epicondyle of the femur and inserts on the bases of the 4 distal phalanges. As its name implies, the extensor digitorum longus extends the phalanges of the hindfoot. Three separate muscles of the peroneus complex, the peroneus longus, the peroneus tertius and the peroneus brevis, can also be found on the lateral surface of the distal hindlimb near the tibialis cranialis. The **peroneus longus** and **peroneus tertius** flex the hindfoot, while the **peroneus brevis** extends the hindfoot. One of the most prominent muscles of the distal portion of the hindlimb is the calf muscle, or **gastrocnemius**. From this aspect, the lateral head of this muscle is visible. The gastrocnemius originates on the femur and inserts on the calcaneus, extending the hindfoot when it contracts. Finally, locate the **tibialis caudalis**, the most caudal of the muscles on the lateral aspect of the distal hindlimb. This muscle originates on the head of the fibula and caudal surface of the tibia and inserts on the metatarsals. Its main role is also to extend the hindfoot.

FIG. 3.22. *Superficial muscles of the lateral aspect of the right distal hindlimb.*

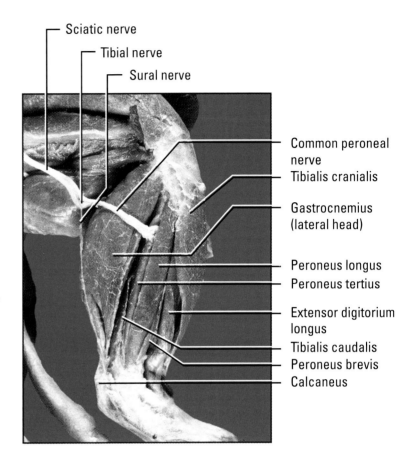

TABLE 3.17. *Superficial muscles of the lateral aspect of the distal hindlimb. Refer to Figure 3.22.*

MUSCLE NAME	ORIGIN	INSERTION	ACTION
Tibialis cranialis	Lateral shaft of tibia and medial shaft of fibula	1st metatarsal	Flexes hindfoot, extends second digit and rotates paw laterally
Extensor digitorum longus	Lateral epicondyle of femur	Bases of the four distal phalanges	Extends phalanges
Peroneus longus	Head of fibula shaft	Proximal ends of all five metatarsals	Flexes hindfoot, abducts and everts
Peroneus tertius	Lateral surface of fibula	1st phalanx of 5th digit	Flexes and everts hindfoot
Peroneus brevis	Distal half of fibula	Tubercle of 5th metatarsal	Extends hindfoot
Gastrocnemius, lateral head	Lateral sesamoid bone of femur	Calcaneus	Extend hindfoot
Tibialis caudalis	Head of fibula and caudal surface of tibia	Metatarsals	Extends hindfoot

Superficial Medial Musculature

Examine the medial aspect of the distal portion of the right hindlimb of your mink (Figure 3.23 and Table 3.18). Some of the same muscles that were visible from the lateral aspect can be seen from the medial side (e.g., tibialis cranialis, tibialis caudalis and gastrocnemius). Three muscles that were not visible from the lateral aspect are the flexor digitorum longus, the flexor digitorum superficialis and the popliteus. As their names suggest, the **flexor digitorum longus** and **flexor digitorum superficialis** both insert on the distal phalanges of the foot and flex the hindfoot. The **popliteus** originates from the lateral epicondyle of the femur and inserts on the tibia. This muscle flexes the knee joint and rotates the hindlimb inward (pronates hindlimb).

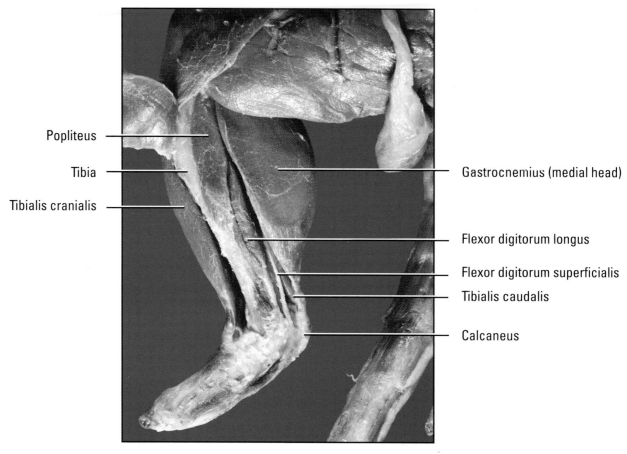

Popliteus

Tibia

Tibialis cranialis

Gastrocnemius (medial head)

Flexor digitorum longus

Flexor digitorum superficialis

Tibialis caudalis

Calcaneus

▲ **FIG. 3.23.** *Superficial muscles of the medial aspect of the right distal hindlimb.*

TABLE 3.18. *Superficial muscles of the medial aspect of the distal hindlimb. Refer to Figure 3.23.*

MUSCLE NAME	ORIGIN	INSERTION	ACTION
Gastrocnemius, medial head	Medial sesamoid bone of femur	Calcaneus	Extends hindfoot
Flexor digitorum longus	Head of fibula and caudal surface of tibia	Distal phalanges of the four digits	Flexes hindfoot
Flexor digitorum superficialis	Broad tendon of calcaneus	Distal end of the four phalanges	Flexes middle phalanges of the digits
Popliteus	Lateral epicondyle of femur	Ventral and medial surface of tibia	Flexes knee joint, rotates hindlimb inward

Digestive System

4

LABORATORY OBJECTIVES

After completing this chapter, you should be able to:

1. Identify the major digestive organs of the mink.

2. Describe the functions of all indicated structures.

3. Identify the digestive enzymes produced by the digestive glands and describe their functions.

4. Recognize the microanatomy of digestive organ tissues.

The digestive system is responsible for mechanically and chemically breaking down food into smaller, usable compounds and then transporting those nutrients into the bloodstream for delivery to the individual cells of the body. This process provides the crucial raw materials and energy for all metabolic processes carried out by the organism. The extreme specialization of individual digestive organs and the efficiency of the digestive process permits mammals to sustain high metabolic rates and maintain an endothermic balance without the need for constant consumption of food.

HEAD, NECK AND ORAL CAVITY

INSTRUCTION

Lay your mink on its side and observe the salivary glands in the neck region that were exposed when you removed the skin around the neck to view the musculature earlier. These structures lay just below the skin and may have been destroyed when dissecting the muscles if caution was not exercised to keep them intact. If so, use the other side of the neck and carefully remove the fat and fascia from around this region to expose these glands (Figure 4.1).

Locate the **parotid gland**, the largest of the salivary glands in the mink (Figure 4.1). Locate the parotid duct emanating from the rostral end of this gland. The **parotid duct** carries digestive enzymes from the parotid gland into the oral cavity where they mix with food. Below and caudal to the parotid gland is the **mandibular gland** which produces saliva. This gland lies just caudal to the digastric muscle which can be seen from a lateral view of the head. Saliva plays an important role in the digestive process of mammals by lubricating the food and starting the digestive reactions. In humans and a few other mammals, **amylase** is released by these glands and is responsible for the breakdown of starches.

Notice the different types of teeth contained within the mouth (Figure 4.2). Minks have a very specialized dentition adapted for their carnivorous lifestyle The **incisors** in the front of the mouth are designed to nip and tear small bites of flesh from their prey. Long, sharp, conical **canines** evolved to puncture flesh and hold struggling prey, while the jagged, razor-sharp **premolars, carnassials** and **molars** are designed to shear away large chunks of flesh, tear through tendons and crush bone.

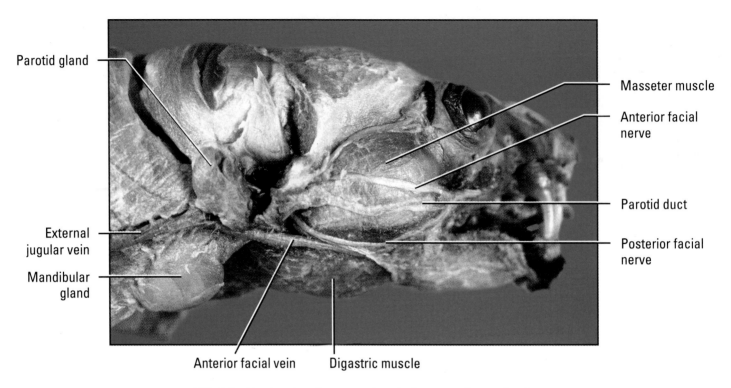

Parotid gland

Masseter muscle

Anterior facial nerve

Parotid duct

External jugular vein

Posterior facial nerve

Mandibular gland

Anterior facial vein   Digastric muscle

▲ **FIG. 4.1.** *Head and neck region of mink showing salivary glands.*

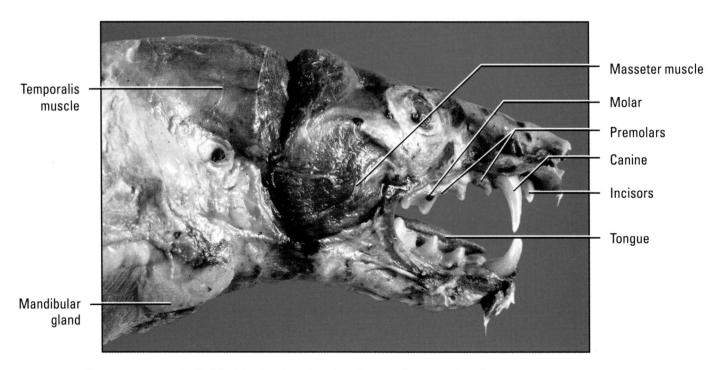

Temporalis muscle

Masseter muscle

Molar

Premolars

Canine

Incisors

Mandibular gland

Tongue

▲ **FIG. 4.2.** *Head and neck region showing diversity of teeth structure.*

TABLE 4.1. *Digestive organs in the mink and their functions. Structures denoted with an asterisk (*) are accessory digestive organs. Food does not pass directly into these accessory organs; however, they do play a major role in the digestive process.*

ORGAN STRUCTURE	FUNCTION
Teeth	Mechanically breakdown food
Salivary glands	Secrete digestive enzymes (e.g., amylase) to begin chemical breakdown of foods and lubricate food for swallowing
Esophagus	Transports food to stomach
Stomach	Produces hydrochloric acid and pepsinogen that aid in the chemical breakdown of food
Duodenum	Receives chyme from the stomach along with secretory enzymes from the gallbladder and pancreas
Liver*	Produces bile, converts glucose to glycogen for storage, detoxifies many constituents of the absorbed digested compounds
Gallbladder*	Stores bile for delivery to duodenum for breakdown of fats
Pancreas*	Produces digestive enzymes and delivers them through pancreatic duct to duodenum
Jejunum	Responsible for majority of nutrient absorption and reabsorption of water
Ileum	Continues process of nutrient absorption and reabsorption of water
Cecum	Has a reduced appearance and function in carnivores and omnivores. In herbivores, this structure is quite large and contains anaerobic bacteria responsible for fermentation of cellulose and other plant materials.
Colon	Responsible for reabsorption of water and electrolytes; produces feces
Rectum	Final site of water reabsorption and feces dehydration
Anus	Regulates egestion of undigested food (feces) from the body

INSTRUCTION

Using your scalpel, make a cut from the corner of the mouth toward the ear on each side of the mink's head. This will extend the opening of the mouth and allow you to view the structures associated with the oral cavity. Don't be afraid to cut too far; usually if you cannot see the structures indicated in the diagram (Figure 4.3), you have not cut far enough. Be sure to angle your incisions so that they continue along the opening to the oral cavity.

In the upper region of the mouth, the roof is comprised of a bony **hard palate** separating the oral cavity from the nasal cavity above (Figure 4.3). The **soft palate** is a continuation caudally from the hard palate. This structure is more fleshy in its consistency than the hard palate. Just caudal to the soft palate is the opening to the **nasopharynx**. This chamber leads rostrally to the external nares. The opening to the **esophagus** should be visible. Next, locate the **glottis**, the opening into the larynx. When a mammal swallows, this opening is protected by a thin flap of cartilage called the **epiglottis**. Slowly close the oral cavity and notice how the epiglottis perfectly meets the opening to the nasopharynx. On the lower jaw, locate the **tongue**. Notice that there are small bumps near the tip and base of the tongue. These are called **papillae** and they help mammals manipulate food in their mouths. Three types of papillae exist, mainly categorized by their respective shapes and location in the mouth. **Fungiform papillae** are found near the front of the tongue, **filiform papillae** are found further back on the tongue, and **vallate papillae** are found near the very rear of the tongue (near the epiglottis) (Figure 4.3A).

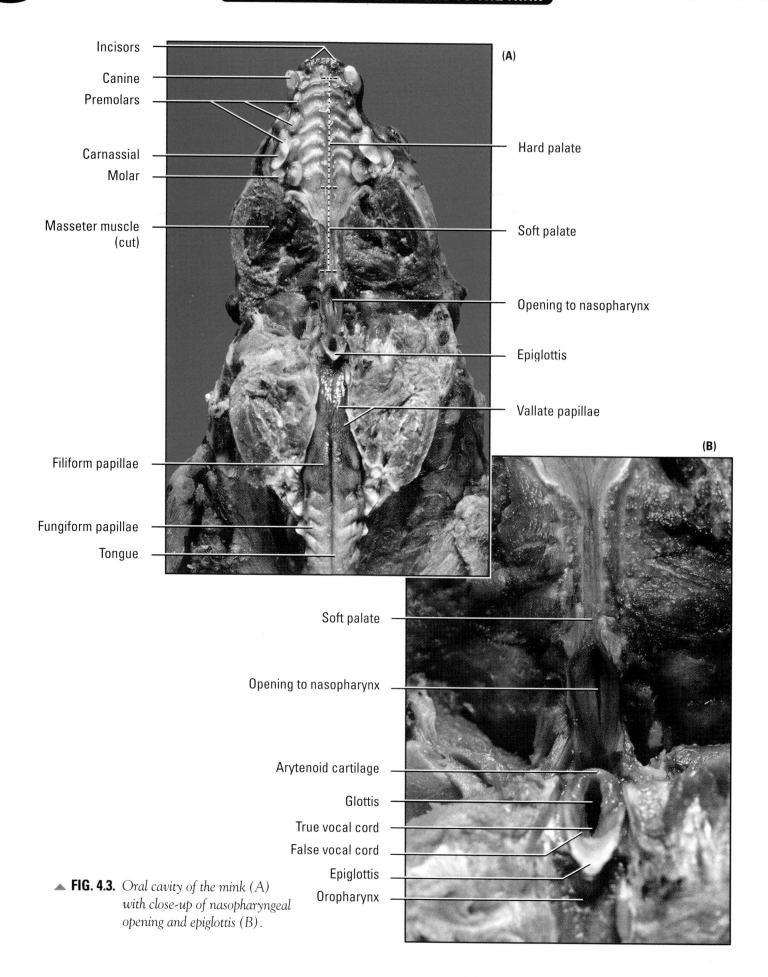

Incisors

Canine

Premolars

Carnassial

Molar

Masseter muscle
(cut)

Hard palate

Soft palate

Opening to nasopharynx

Epiglottis

Vallate papillae

Filiform papillae

Fungiform papillae

Tongue

(A)

(B)

Soft palate

Opening to nasopharynx

Arytenoid cartilage

Glottis

True vocal cord

False vocal cord

Epiglottis

Oropharynx

▲ **FIG. 4.3.** *Oral cavity of the mink* (A)
*with close-up of nasopharyngeal
opening and epiglottis* (B).

ABDOMINAL CAVITY

When you first open the abdominal cavity, the majority of organs below the liver will be covered by a thin, membranous tissue layer known as the **greater omentum** (Figure 4.5A). This tissue is a fragile, double-layered, specialized mesentery that holds the abdominal organs in place by attaching them to each other and to the walls of the peritoneal cavity.

A thin muscular layer (the diaphragm) separates the upper thoracic cavity from the lower abdominal cavity (Figures 4.4B–4.6). The role of the diaphragm will be discussed in Chapter 6. For now, you should concentrate your efforts on structures that are in the abdominal cavity only. Food that is swallowed passes down the **esophagus** and into the **stomach**. The esophagus is a narrow tube containing smooth muscle that contracts to push food into the stomach. The stomach lies on the left side of the mink underneath the large, dark liver. It is a J-shaped sac that is responsible for storing large quantities of food. This relieves mammals of the need to eat constantly. A large stomach permits an animal to consume large quantities of food in a very short time span and then retire to a safe place to digest the meal over several hours. The stomach releases several chemical compounds that assist the digestive process including **hydrochloric acid** and **pepsinogen**.

Notice that there are small folds on the inside of the stomach wall. These are called **rugae**, and they help churn the food and mix it with chemical secretions. The stomach empties its contents into the **duodenum** – the first portion of the small intestine. At this point, several accessory glands empty digestive fluids into the duodenum. Locate the **liver**, the largest organ in the abdominal region. In the mink, the liver has five distinct lobes (Figure 4.6). The liver is a multi-functional organ that contributes to many systems in the body. One function of the liver is to produce bile which is stored in the **gallbladder**. The gallbladder is located on the underside of the right median lobe of the liver (Figures 4.7–4.8). **Bile** contains no digestive enzymes, but it does contain bile salts which assist in the breakdown of fats. The bile is released from the gallbladder directly into the **cystic duct** which carries the bile into the **common bile duct** and then into the duodenum.

Now locate the **pancreas**, a whitish-yellow, elongated, granular organ imbedded in the mesenteries that support the stomach (Figure 4.6). The pancreas is actually composed of two lobes, a left lobe which runs transversely across the body and a smaller, right lobe which runs longitudinally along the length of the duodenum (Figure 4.9). The pancreas produces several kinds of digestive enzymes and hormones. The digestive enzymes empty into the duodenum via the small **pancreatic duct** (Figure 4.9B).

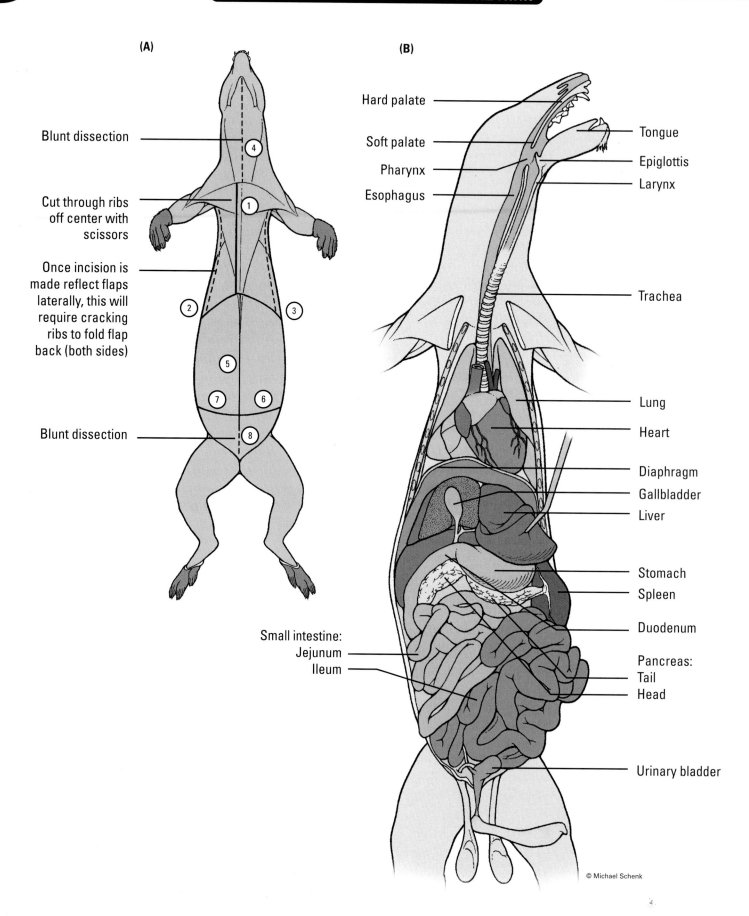

(A)

Blunt dissection

Cut through ribs off center with scissors

Once incision is made reflect flaps laterally, this will require cracking ribs to fold flap back (both sides)

Blunt dissection

(B)

Hard palate

Soft palate

Pharynx

Esophagus

Tongue

Epiglottis

Larynx

Trachea

Lung

Heart

Diaphragm

Gallbladder

Liver

Stomach

Spleen

Duodenum

Pancreas:
Tail
Head

Small intestine:
Jejunum
Ileum

Urinary bladder

© Michael Schenk

▲ **FIG. 4.4.** *Diagram of incisions for exposing internal organs (A). Internal organs of the thoracic and abdominal cavity (B).*

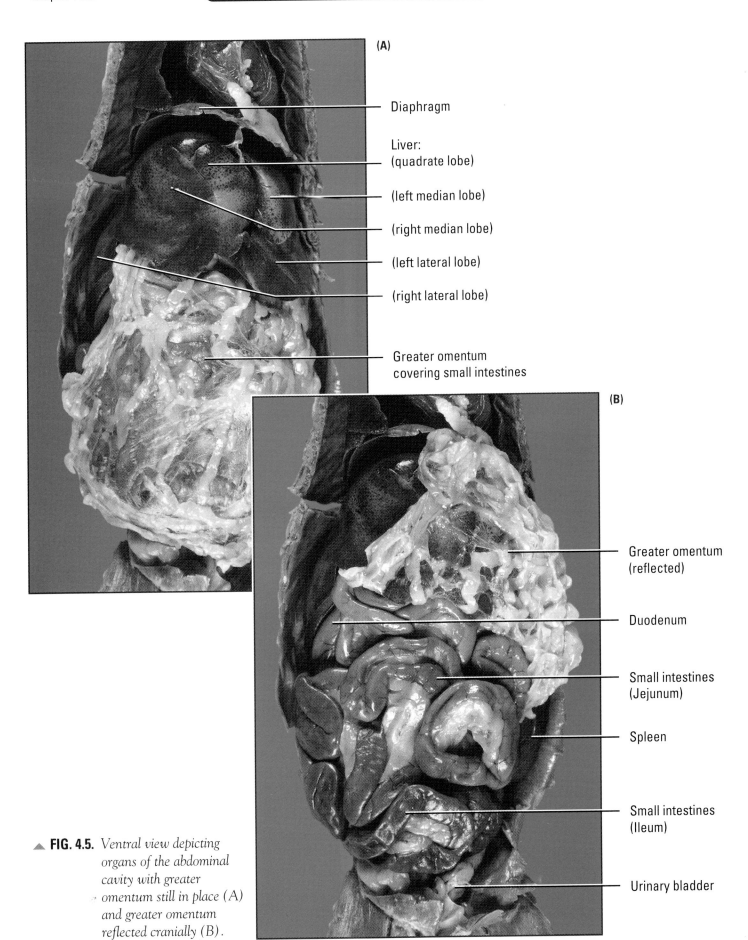

(A)

Diaphragm

Liver:
(quadrate lobe)

(left median lobe)

(right median lobe)

(left lateral lobe)

(right lateral lobe)

Greater omentum
covering small intestines

(B)

Greater omentum
(reflected)

Duodenum

Small intestines
(Jejunum)

Spleen

Small intestines
(Ileum)

Urinary bladder

▲ **FIG. 4.5.** *Ventral view depicting
organs of the abdominal
cavity with greater
omentum still in place (A)
and greater omentum
reflected cranially (B).*

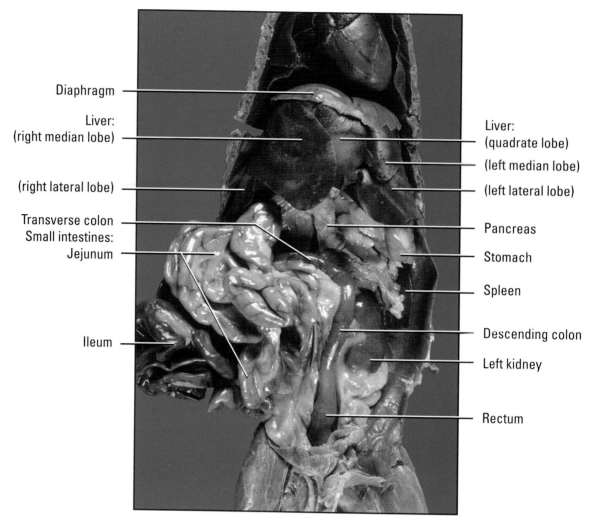

Diaphragm

Liver:
(right median lobe)

(right lateral lobe)

Transverse colon
Small intestines:
Jejunum

Ileum

Liver:
(quadrate lobe)

(left median lobe)

(left lateral lobe)

Pancreas

Stomach

Spleen

Descending colon

Left kidney

Rectum

▲ **FIG. 4.6.** *Lobes of the liver and other digestive organs; small intestine has been reflected cranially to expose descending colon and rectum.*

The duodenum receives the partially digested foodstuffs and enzyme mix, known as **chyme**, from the stomach and is primarily responsible for the final stages of enzymatic digestion. Food passes next into the **jejunum**. This region of the small intestine is highly convoluted and tightly bound together by **mesentery**. Absorption of nutrients and water occurs along the length of the jejunum and the nutrients are delivered to the circulatory system through the hundreds of small blood vessels found throughout the intestinal mesentery. If your mink has been injected, these blood vessels should be readily apparent. Chyme continues into the distal portion of the small intestine known as the **ileum** where further nutrient absorption and water reabsorption occur. Again, there are more blood vessels associated with the mesentery of this region to deliver the nutrients to the circulatory system. At the juncture of the small intestine and the tightly-coiled colon there is a short, blind-ended pocket of the intestine known as the **cecum**. In carnivores and omnivores the cecum is very small and does not play a large role in digestion. However,

in herbivores the cecum is typically quite large and serves as a fermentation chamber where symbiotic bacteria break down cellulose and other plant matter. The mixture passes next through the **colon** which is primarily responsible for reabsorption of water. In many mammals, the colon is divided into three regions based on their positions in the body: the **ascending colon**, the **transverse colon** and the **descending colon**. Functionally they are identical. Locate the descending portion of the colon that runs along the dorsal aspect of the abdominal cavity. Its distal portion is referred to as the **rectum**. The colon and rectum permit mammals to conserve valuable water and produce a dry feces. From the beginning of the digestive process, fluid-based chemicals have been mixed in with the food. At this point, most usable nutrients have been dissolved and absorbed by the duodenum, jejunum and ileum, and the water that was previously added is now reabsorbed. The undigested food particles (feces) are finally egested from the body through the **anus** in a process known as defecation—not excretion!

◀ **FIG. 4.7.** *Illustration of isolated digestive system.*

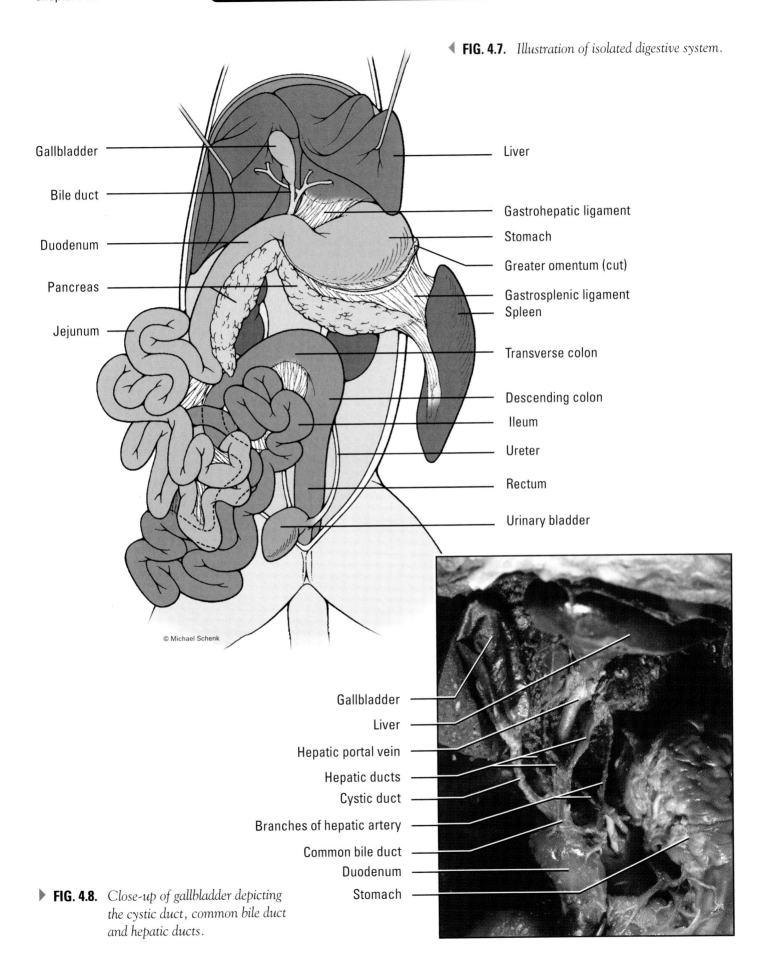

Gallbladder

Bile duct

Duodenum

Pancreas

Jejunum

Liver

Gastrohepatic ligament

Stomach

Greater omentum (cut)

Gastrosplenic ligament

Spleen

Transverse colon

Descending colon

Ileum

Ureter

Rectum

Urinary bladder

© Michael Schenk

Gallbladder

Liver

Hepatic portal vein

Hepatic ducts

Cystic duct

Branches of hepatic artery

Common bile duct

Duodenum

Stomach

▶ **FIG. 4.8.** *Close-up of gallbladder depicting the cystic duct, common bile duct and hepatic ducts.*

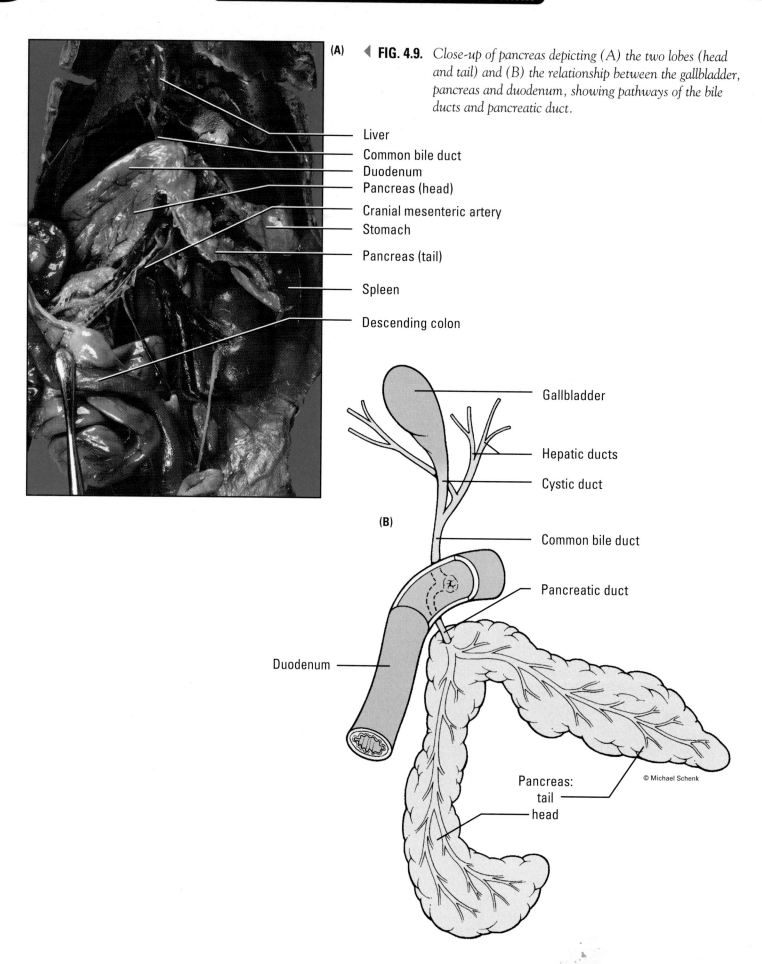

(A)

FIG. 4.9. *Close-up of pancreas depicting (A) the two lobes (head and tail) and (B) the relationship between the gallbladder, pancreas and duodenum, showing pathways of the bile ducts and pancreatic duct.*

Liver

Common bile duct

Duodenum

Pancreas (head)

Cranial mesenteric artery

Stomach

Pancreas (tail)

Spleen

Descending colon

Gallbladder

Hepatic ducts

Cystic duct

(B)

Common bile duct

Pancreatic duct

Duodenum

Pancreas:
tail
head

© Michael Schenk

CHAPTER 5

Circulatory System

LABORATORY OBJECTIVES

After completing this chapter, you should be able to:

1. Identify the major arteries and veins of the mink.
2. Identify the chambers and internal anatomy of the heart.
3. Discuss the function of all indicated structures.
4. Discuss the circulatory pathway of blood in the mammalian system.

The circulatory (or cardiovascular) system is responsible for transporting nutrients, gases, hormones and metabolic wastes to and from the individual cells of an organism. Mammals are far too large for all of their individual cells to exchange nutrients, wastes and gases with the external world by simple diffusion. Most cells are buried too deep inside the body to effectively accomplish this task. Thus, some system must be in place to efficiently exchange these products between the outside world and every cell in the organism's body. For this reason, the circulatory system is a highly-branched network of vessels that spreads throughout the entire organism. In general the circulatory system represents a series of vessels that diverge from the heart (arteries) to supply blood to the tissues and a confluence of vessels draining blood from the tissues and returning it to the heart (veins). Despite the extensive network of arteries and veins throughout the body, no actual exchange of water, nutrients, wastes or gases occurs in arteries or veins. Their walls are too thick to permit diffusion. Extensive networks of capillary beds connecting branches of arteries and veins exist throughout the body to transfer these dissolved substances between the bloodstream and the tissues.

To simplify identification of the numerous arteries and veins, there are two general principles you should remember: (1) arteries and veins tend to be paired, especially when the organs they supply or drain are paired, and (2) a continuous vessel often undergoes several name changes along its length as it passes through different regions. Therefore to successfully identify arteries and veins it is necessary to trace them along their entire length (typically from the heart outward).

THORACIC CAVITY AND NECK REGION

Notice the thin **pericardial membrane** surrounding the heart (Figure 5.1A). This protective sac contains a small amount of lubricating fluid to protect the heart and cushion its movements. You should see several arteries and veins emerging from the pericardial membrane. This membrane fits snugly against these arteries and veins and must be carefully removed to fully view these vessels and the other regions of the heart itself. If your dissection was performed carefully, you should see the **right internal mammary artery** (sometimes called the cranial epigastric or internal thoracic artery) and the common trunk of the **internal mammary veins** extending from the confluence of blood vessels located a few centimeters cranial to the heart. These minute vessels supply blood to the tissues of the ventral surface of the rib cage and return blood to the heart from the intercostal tissues. Due to their small size, they are easily damaged during dissection if great care is not taken when opening the thoracic cavity.

Veins of the Thoracic Region

Reflection of the heart to either side will reveal the **pulmonary arteries** and the **pulmonary veins**, the vessels that carry deoxygenated blood from the right ventricle to the lungs and return oxygenated blood to the left atrium of the heart (Figure 5.2). Because the blood that flows through the pulmonary arteries is deoxygenated, these vessels are injected with blue latex (unlike the other arteries in the body). Likewise, the pulmonary veins are injected with red latex, since they carry oxygenated blood. Do not let the color difference confuse your identification of these vessels.

The largest veins in mammals are the **cranial vena cava** and **caudal vena cava**, which converge at the entrance to the right atrium (Figures 5.2–5.4). These two large, thin-walled veins bring deoxygenated blood back to the heart from all parts of the body. Trace the cranial vena cava cranially to its first major branch (past the branch of the internal mammary trunk. Here several smaller veins converge on the cranial vena cava at a junction known as the **brachiocephalic trunk**. Remember blood is flowing back *toward the heart* through these vessels. In the mink, the brachiocephalic trunk is extremely short and does not contain prominent right and left branches, as in many other mammals. The veins leading into the brachiocephalic trunk are symmetrically arranged in the right and left halves of the body, so each vein has a corresponding member in the other half of the thoracic cavity (e.g., left internal jugular and right internal jugular veins). For purposes of clarity, we have not labeled every corresponding vein on each side of the body in the diagrams. Use each "half" of a diagram to identify all of the vessels discussed in the text.

Four major veins converge on the brachiocephalic trunk (Figures 5.3–5.4). The pair of veins draining blood from the lateral portions of the thoracic cavity and forelimbs are the **left and right subclavian veins**. Follow the right subclavian vein distally. A small vein branches off the subclavian vein and leads cranially. This is the **ventral thoracic vein**. After this branching point, the subclavian vein "becomes" the **axillary vein**. Another small branch can be found further distally, this time branching caudally. It is the **long thoracic vein**. The distal portion of the axillary vein from this branch is known as the **brachial vein** as it proceeds into the forelimb.

The other pair of veins converging on the brachiocephalic trunk come from the head and neck region. The **right and left external jugular veins** extend from the brachiocephalic trunk cranially along the outer margins of the neck to the head. Very near their junction with the

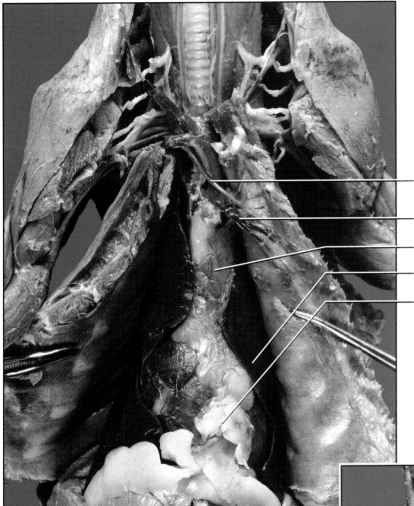

FIG. 5.1. *Heart surrounded by pericardial membrane (A), heart with pericardial membrane removed (B) and histology photograph of artery and vein (C).*

Right internal mammary artery
(internal thoracic or cranial epigastric)

Common trunk of internal mammary veins

Thymus

Left lung

Heart encased in pericardium

(A)

(B)

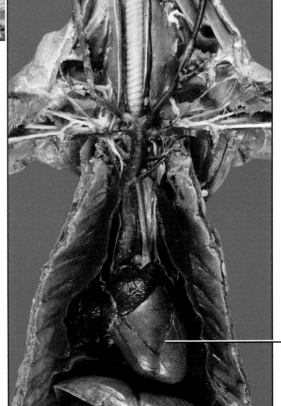

Heart
(Pericardium
and thymus
removed)

(C)

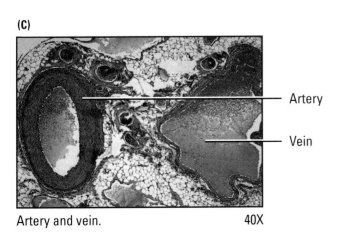

Artery

Vein

Artery and vein.   40X

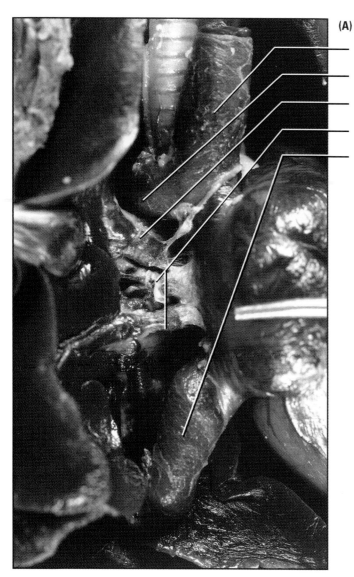

(A)

Cranial vena cava
Azygos vein
Right pulmonary artery
Right pulmonary veins
Caudal vena cava

Cranial vena cava
Aorta
RA
LA
RV
LV
Caudal vena cava
Aorta
(C)
© Michael Schenk

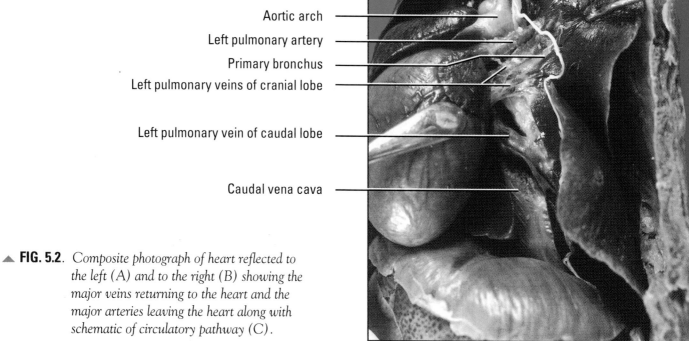

(B)

Aortic arch
Left pulmonary artery
Primary bronchus
Left pulmonary veins of cranial lobe

Left pulmonary vein of caudal lobe

Caudal vena cava

▲ **FIG. 5.2**. *Composite photograph of heart reflected to the left (A) and to the right (B) showing the major veins returning to the heart and the major arteries leaving the heart along with schematic of circulatory pathway (C).*

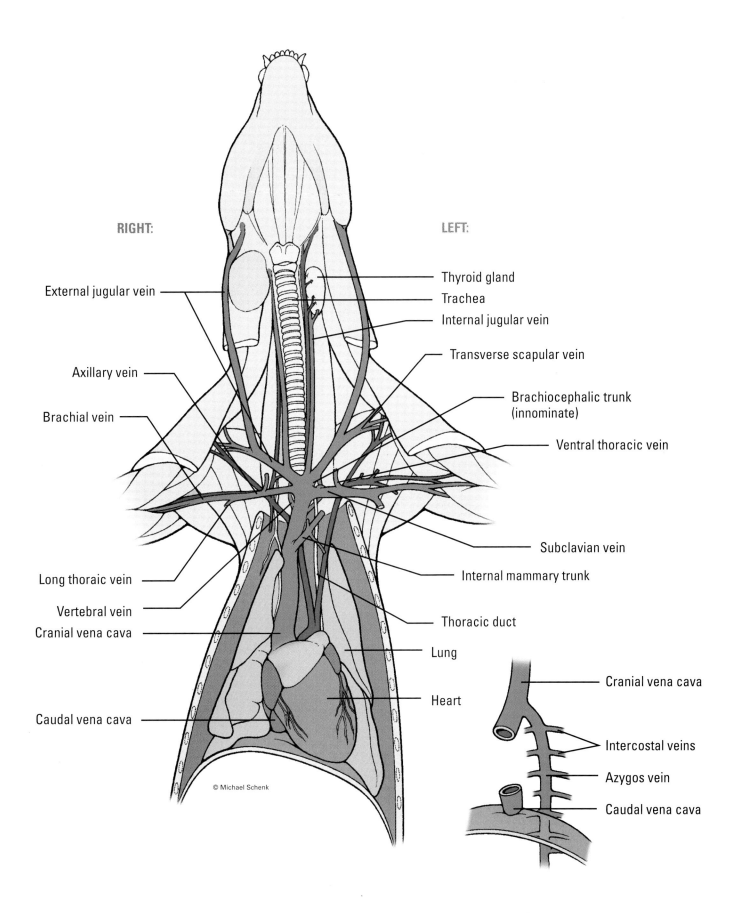

RIGHT:

LEFT:

External jugular vein

Axillary vein

Brachial vein

Long thoraic vein

Vertebral vein

Cranial vena cava

Caudal vena cava

Thyroid gland

Trachea

Internal jugular vein

Transverse scapular vein

Brachiocephalic trunk (innominate)

Ventral thoracic vein

Subclavian vein

Internal mammary trunk

Thoracic duct

Lung

Heart

Cranial vena cava

Intercostal veins

Azygos vein

Caudal vena cava

© Michael Schenk

▲ **FIG. 5.3.** *Illustration of thoracic veins; position of azygos vein depicted in inset.*

▶ **FIG. 5.4.** *Thoracic veins—ventral view (A) and right lateral view (B).*

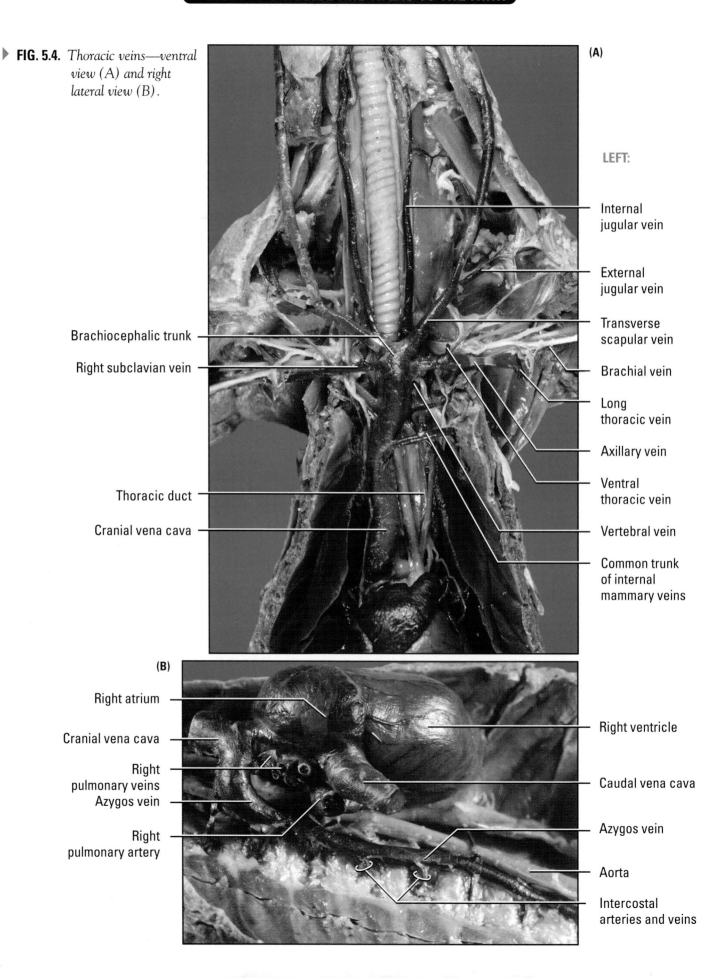

(A)

LEFT:

Internal jugular vein

External jugular vein

Transverse scapular vein

Brachial vein

Long thoracic vein

Axillary vein

Ventral thoracic vein

Vertebral vein

Common trunk of internal mammary veins

Brachiocephalic trunk

Right subclavian vein

Thoracic duct

Cranial vena cava

(B)

Right atrium

Cranial vena cava

Right pulmonary veins

Azygos vein

Right pulmonary artery

Right ventricle

Caudal vena cava

Azygos vein

Aorta

Intercostal arteries and veins

brachiocephalic trunk, you should see the location where the **right and left internal jugular veins** connect to the external jugular veins. Together, these veins drain deoxygenated blood from the head and neck of the mink. Follow the right external jugular vein cranially past its juncture with the right internal jugular vein to another branch leading to the shoulder. The **transverse scapular vein** joins the external jugular vein at this point. Finally, reflect the heart to one side and locate the **azygos vein** (Figure 5.4B) that courses along the dorsal surface of the thoracic cavity and joins the cranial vena cava very near the heart. This vessel drains blood from the dorsal tissues of the rib cage. Humans possess both an azygos vein on the right side of the body and a hemiazygos vein on the left that are interconnected by numerous vessels.

INSTRUCTION

You may find it helpful to remove veins from the thoracic region to better view the arteries in this area. If so, proceed with care. Only remove veins that you have identified and be careful not to damage arteries in the process. Since many veins lie adjacent to neighboring arteries, you will need to exercise caution when removing the veins.

Arteries of the Thoracic Region

Follow the pulmonary artery from the right ventricle around and behind the heart and observe where it branches into the **right and left pulmonary arteries**—the arteries responsible for delivering deoxygenated blood to the lungs (REMEMBER: they will probably be injected with blue latex!). Now locate the **aorta** leaving the left ventricle. The aorta curves to the left as it leaves the left ventricle, branches twice (in the mink) and continues caudally along the dorsal body wall, passing through the diaphragm into the abdominal cavity. The first major branch of the aorta is the **brachiocephalic artery** which passes obliquely and cranially toward the right side of the thoracic region (Figures 5.5–5.6). The brachiocephalic artery diverges into the **right subclavian artery** and the **left common carotid**. The **right common carotid artery** branches off the right subclavian artery further cranially along its length. Together the common carotid arteries supply oxygenated blood to the head and neck.

The second major branch from the aorta is the **left subclavian artery**. Together the subclavian arteries supply oxygenated blood to the forelimbs. The subclavian arteries exhibit extensive branching once they reach the cranial boundaries of the rib cage. Very thin **internal mammary arteries** (leading into the chest) and larger **vertebral arter-**

ies (leading dorsally) should be visible on each side in this area. Larger branches of the subclavian arteries are the **right and left axillary arteries** and the **right and left thyrocervical arteries**. The **right and left subscapular arteries** (leading cranially) and the **right and left long thoracic arteries** (leading caudally) branch from the axillary arteries. Collectively, the subscapular arteries and thyrocervical arteries carry blood to the shoulders. After this branching point, the axillary artery becomes the **brachial artery** as it leads distally into the forelimb.

INSTRUCTION

Carefully remove the mandibular gland and cut away the digastric muscle from the left side of the neck to expose the underlying blood vessels. Remove any other muscles that still obscure your view of the larynx and the nearby blood vessels. Leave the thyroid gland on the left side of the neck in place and do not cut through any arteries or veins while removing these structures.

Arteries of the Neck

Follow the left common carotid artery cranially to the thyroid gland. Using a blunt probe, reflect the thyroid gland laterally to expose two arteries (and corresponding veins) branching off the common carotid and leading into the thyroid gland (Figure 5.7). These are the **cranial and caudal thyroid arteries**. Trace the common carotid further cranially to the point where a branch known as the **laryngeal artery** supplies blood to the larynx. Shortly after this branch, near the base of the jaw, the common carotid artery branches into the short **external carotid artery** and the **lingual artery**, the latter running cranially along the hypoglossal nerve for a short distance before becoming embedded in the deep musculature. The right and left lingual arteries are the main suppliers of blood to the tongue, while the external carotids carry blood further along the head. Dissection cranially will reveal that the external carotid artery immediately branches to form the **internal maxillary artery** and the **external maxillary artery** which supply blood to the facial region.

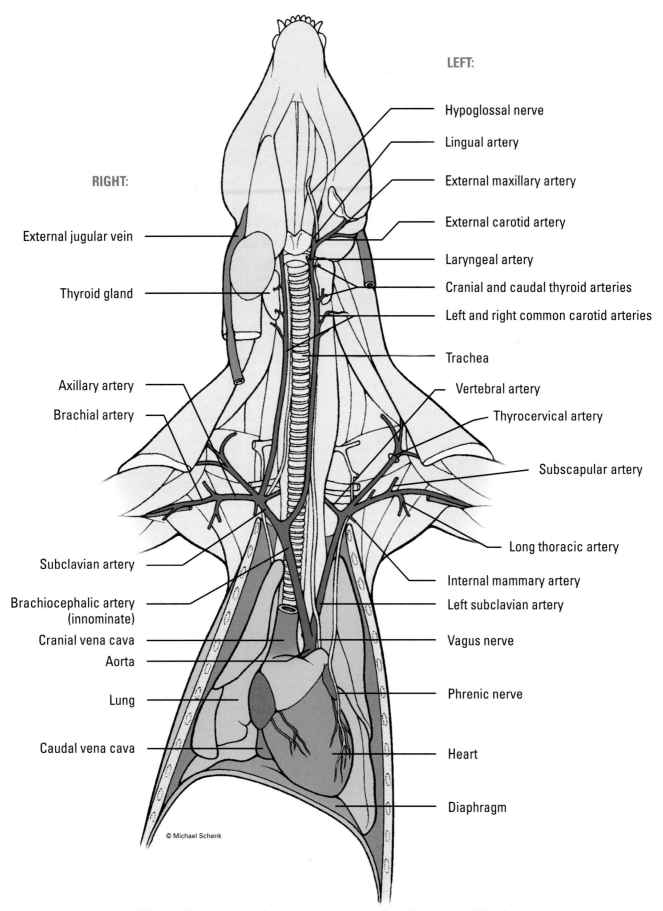

LEFT:

RIGHT:

Hypoglossal nerve

Lingual artery

External maxillary artery

External carotid artery

External jugular vein

Laryngeal artery

Cranial and caudal thyroid arteries

Thyroid gland

Left and right common carotid arteries

Trachea

Axillary artery

Vertebral artery

Brachial artery

Thyrocervical artery

Subscapular artery

Long thoracic artery

Subclavian artery

Internal mammary artery

Brachiocephalic artery (innominate)

Left subclavian artery

Cranial vena cava

Vagus nerve

Aorta

Lung

Phrenic nerve

Caudal vena cava

Heart

Diaphragm

© Michael Schenk

▲ **FIG. 5.5.** *Illustration of thoracic arteries (veins have been omitted for clarity).*

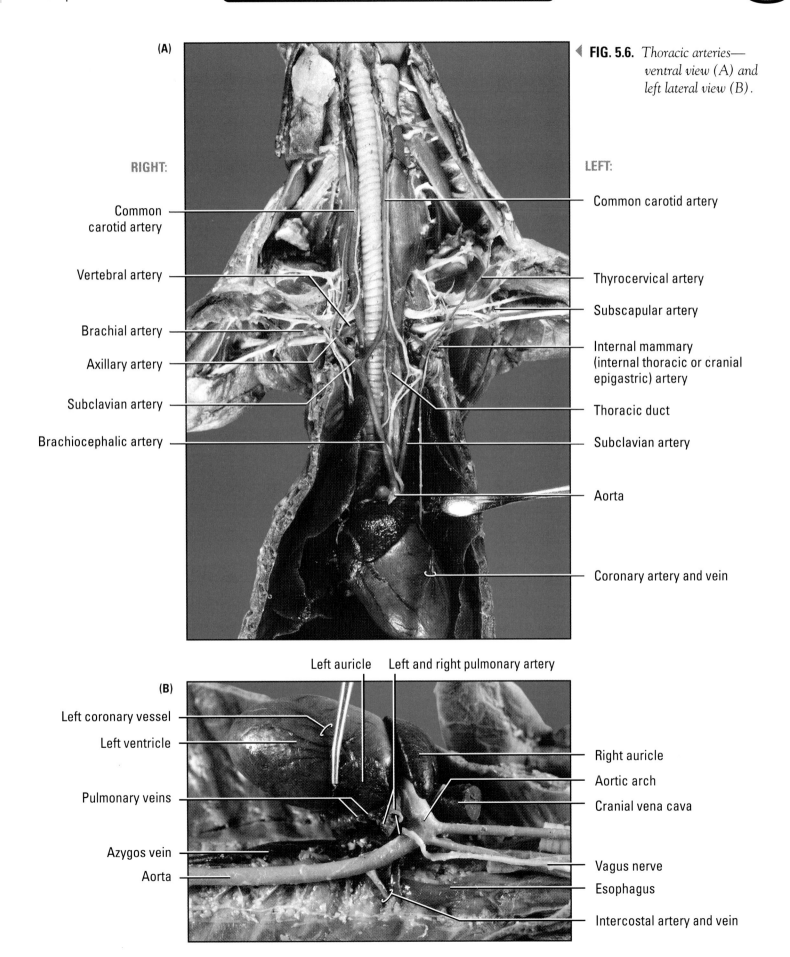

(A)

RIGHT:

Common carotid artery

Vertebral artery

Brachial artery

Axillary artery

Subclavian artery

Brachiocephalic artery

◀ **FIG. 5.6.** *Thoracic arteries— ventral view* (A) *and left lateral view* (B).

LEFT:

Common carotid artery

Thyrocervical artery

Subscapular artery

Internal mammary (internal thoracic or cranial epigastric) artery

Thoracic duct

Subclavian artery

Aorta

Coronary artery and vein

(B)

Left auricle   Left and right pulmonary artery

Left coronary vessel

Left ventricle

Pulmonary veins

Azygos vein

Aorta

Right auricle

Aortic arch

Cranial vena cava

Vagus nerve

Esophagus

Intercostal artery and vein

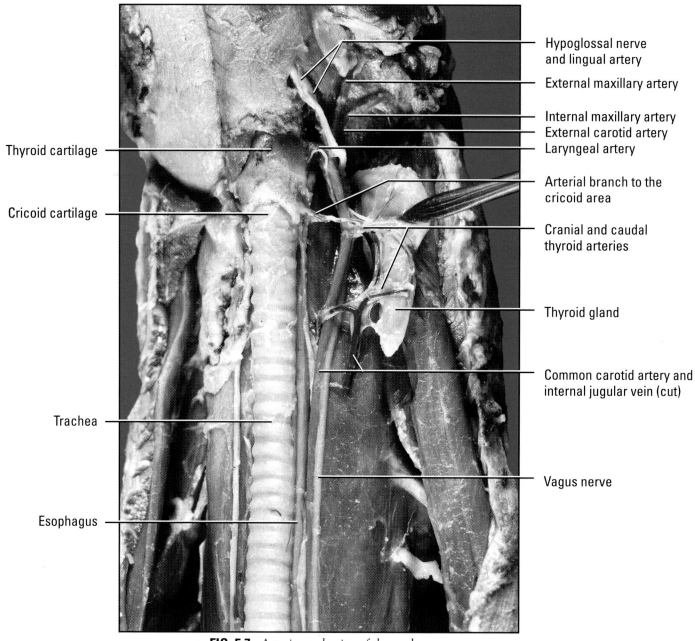

Thyroid cartilage

Cricoid cartilage

Trachea

Esophagus

Hypoglossal nerve
and lingual artery

External maxillary artery

Internal maxillary artery
External carotid artery
Laryngeal artery

Arterial branch to the
cricoid area

Cranial and caudal
thyroid arteries

Thyroid gland

Common carotid artery and
internal jugular vein (cut)

Vagus nerve

▲ **FIG. 5.7.** *Arteries and veins of the neck.*

ABDOMINAL CAVITY

Hepatic Portal System

Follow the **caudal vena cava** from the heart through the diaphragm and liver toward the stomach. Notice how it passes directly through the diaphragm and through the center of the lobes of the liver. Between the liver and stomach there is a unique system of veins called the **hepatic portal system** (Figures 5.8–5.11). Portal systems in general are found in many different parts of the body in mammals. They serve important functions in rerouting blood to special organs before allowing it to pass along to the rest of the body. The difference in circulation between the normal circulatory pathway and the pathway of a portal system is depicted below.

Normal Circulatory Pathway:
artery ▶ capillary bed ▶ vein

Portal System:
artery ▶ capillary bed ▶ portal vein ▶ capillary bed ▶ vein

In the case of the hepatic portal system, blood flows from the capillary beds of the small and large intestines, the spleen, the pancreas and the stomach into the **hepatic portal vein** (Figures 5.8–5.10) and then into the capillary beds of the liver, before entering the caudal vena cava. This extra step allows blood from the stomach and intes-

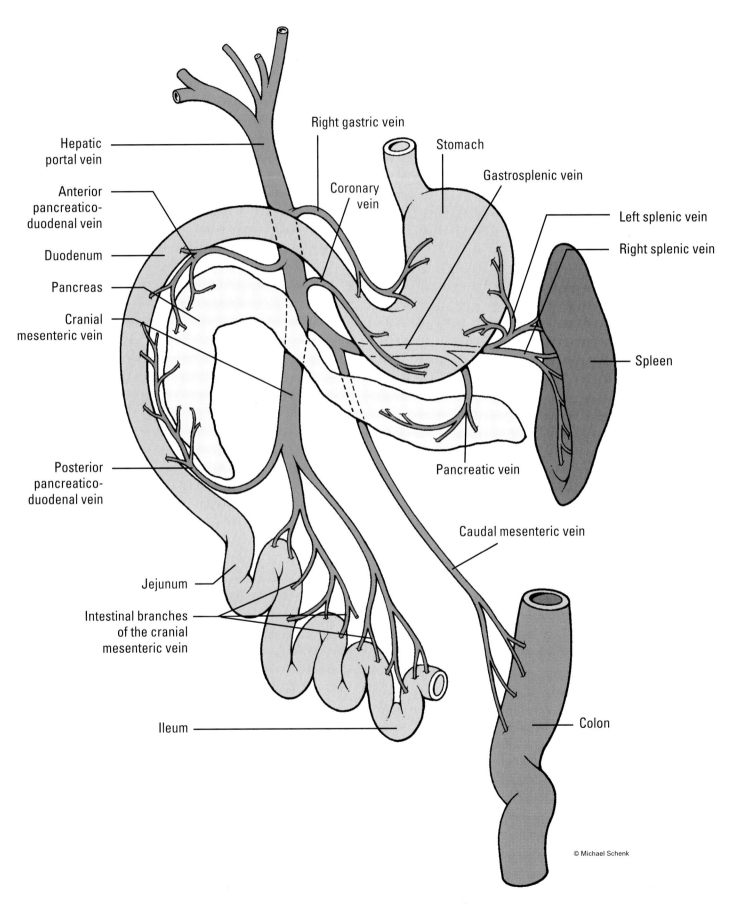

Hepatic portal vein

Anterior pancreatico-duodenal vein

Duodenum

Pancreas

Cranial mesenteric vein

Posterior pancreatico-duodenal vein

Jejunum

Intestinal branches of the cranial mesenteric vein

Ileum

Right gastric vein

Stomach

Coronary vein

Gastrosplenic vein

Left splenic vein

Right splenic vein

Spleen

Pancreatic vein

Caudal mesenteric vein

Colon

© Michael Schenk

FIG. 5.8. *Illustration of hepatic portal system.*

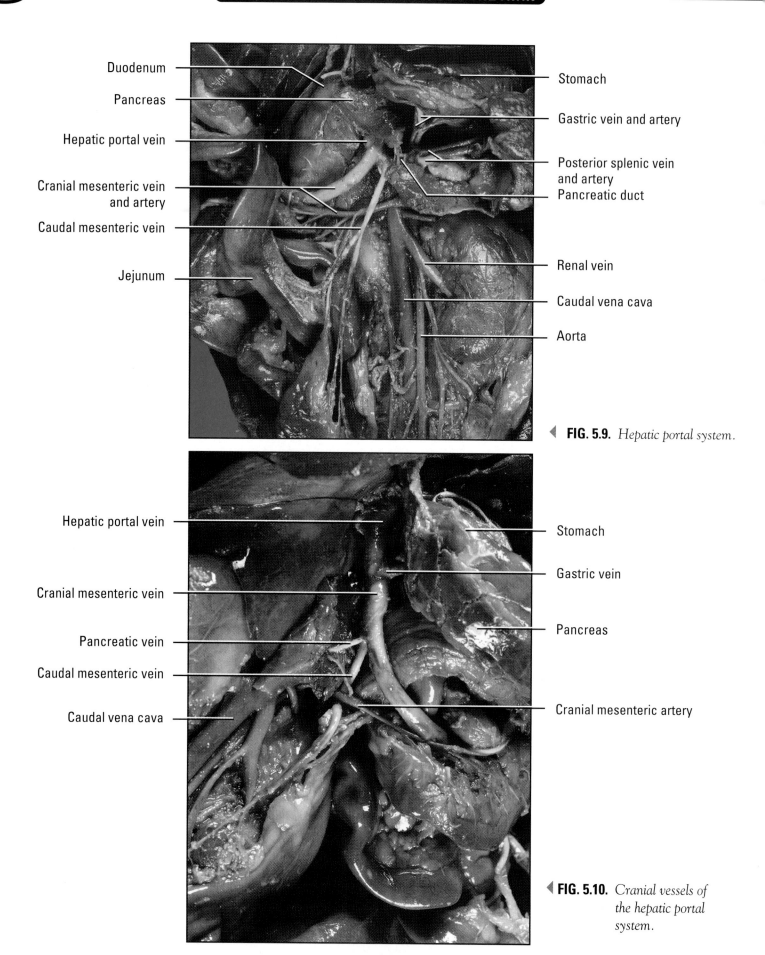

Duodenum

Pancreas

Hepatic portal vein

Cranial mesenteric vein and artery

Caudal mesenteric vein

Jejunum

Stomach

Gastric vein and artery

Posterior splenic vein and artery

Pancreatic duct

Renal vein

Caudal vena cava

Aorta

◀ **FIG. 5.9.** *Hepatic portal system.*

Hepatic portal vein

Cranial mesenteric vein

Pancreatic vein

Caudal mesenteric vein

Caudal vena cava

Stomach

Gastric vein

Pancreas

Cranial mesenteric artery

◀ **FIG. 5.10.** *Cranial vessels of the hepatic portal system.*

tines that contains large amounts of sugars and possibly toxins to be filtered by the liver before the blood is sent to the rest of the body. Also, hormones produced by the pancreas (e.g., insulin, glucagon, somatostatin) can be directed to their target organ, the liver, without the delay of traveling through the entire body first. Depending on the type and amount of hormone released by the pancreas, the liver may store the sugar (as glycogen) or release it into the bloodstream immediately. Through this regulatory mechanism, the liver maintains nearly constant blood glucose levels. Secondly, deleterious compounds are removed from the blood before they reach other organs and possibly harm the body. Occasionally the intake of these toxins (e.g., alcohol) exceeds the rate at which the liver can filter them from the blood, and the excess passes through the bloodstream to other organs. Since the hepatic portal system is "surrounded" by capillary beds, it requires a special injection directly into the vessels for visualization. As a result, specimens will have yellow latex in the veins of the hepatic portal system, facilitating identification of these vessels.

Blood from the lower portion of the duodenum, the coils of the jejunum and the ileum drain into the **cranial mesenteric vein** which becomes the hepatic portal vein further cranially near the liver (Figure 5.9). Veins associated with the colon send their contents through the **caudal mesenteric vein** which fuses with the **gastrosplenic vein**, bringing blood from the stomach and spleen, before joining the cranial mesenteric vein near the base of the stomach (Figure 5.11). Blood from the pancreas and upper region of the duodenum passes through the **anterior and posterior pancreaticoduodenal veins** which both drain into the cranial mesenteric vein. The anterior pancreaticoduodenal vein enters the cranial mesenteric vein near the junction of the **gastric vein** which brings blood from the cranial aspect of the stomach. After the cranial mesenteric vein is joined by the gastric vein, it becomes the hepatic portal vein.

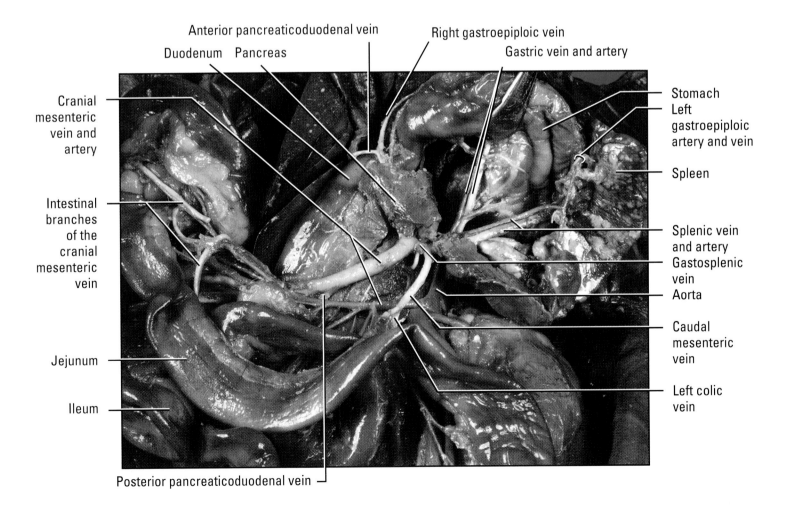

▲ **FIG. 5.11.** *Caudal vessels of the hepatic portal system.*

The Spleen

The **spleen** is a vascular, ductless organ that plays a critical role in the circulatory system of vertebrates. Since mammalian red blood cells do not contain nuclei, they cannot undergo cell division and thus have a finite life span. New red blood cells are continuously produced in the bone marrow and delivered to the spleen for storage. The spleen stores these cells along with excess blood and releases these products into the bloodstream as needed. Through this mechanism the spleen regulates the body's total blood volume and the concentration of red blood cells. The spleen also manufactures white blood cells (lymphocytes) to fend off diseases and destroys and recycles worn-out blood cells (Figure 5.12).

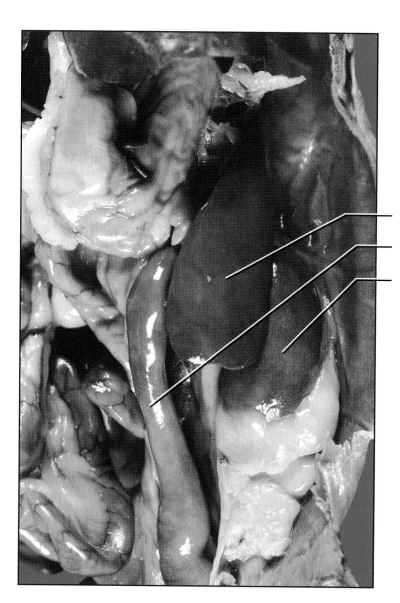

Spleen

Descending colon

Left kidney

▲ **FIG. 5.12.** *Spleen with accompanying histology photograph.*

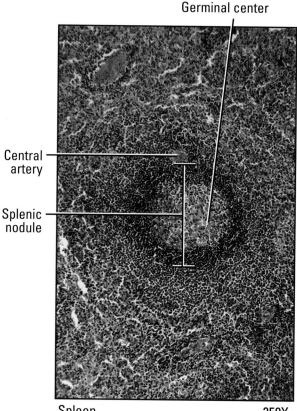

Germinal center

Central artery

Splenic nodule

Spleen.   250X

Arteries and Veins of the Abdominal Region

As the aorta passes caudally through the abdominal region, several more branches arise from it. The first of these is the **celiac artery**, a small branch from the aorta to the stomach, pancreas and spleen (Figures 5.13–5.14). The celiac artery branches into a network of arteries leading into each of these organs. Careful inspection of the organs associated with this network should reveal several arteries: the **hepatic artery** leading into the liver, the **left gastric artery** supplying the stomach and the **splenic artery** carrying blood to the spleen (Figure 5.14B). Next find the **cranial mesenteric artery**. This artery contains branches that supply the jejunum, ileum and colon. Just caudal to the cranial mesenteric artery, the **adrenolumbar arteries and veins** should be visible. These short vessels supply and drain the small adrenal glands and lumbar muscles. The adrenolumbar veins dump their blood directly into the caudal vena cava. The **caudal vena cava** is the primary vein that drains blood from the abdominal cavity and lower extremities of the body. It is a large thin-walled vessel that extends along the length of the dorsal body wall from the caudal portion of the abdomen through the diaphragm and into the right atrium of the heart. Along the way, many other smaller veins send their blood into the caudal vena cava.

INSTRUCTION

Remove the liver and digestive organs of the abdominal cavity by carefully cutting (1) the esophagus near the stomach, (2) the descending colon near the rectum, (3) the hepatic veins connecting the liver to the vena cava, (4) the celiac artery connecting the stomach, pancreas and spleen to the aorta, (5) the cranial mesenteric artery connecting the intestines to the aorta and (6) the caudal mesenteric artery. When cutting arteries and veins, leave a significant portion of the vessel attached to the circulatory system; that is, cut vessels as close as possible to the organs you are removing. Use Figure 5.13 as a guide to exposing the underlying vasculature of the abdominal region.

Further caudally, two short branches of the dorsal aorta lead into the kidneys. These are the **renal arteries**. Lying next to the renal arteries, the thinner-walled **renal veins** are present. These vessels collect filtered blood from the kidneys. The right and left renal veins are slightly offset (as are the kidneys) and do not join the vena cava at exactly the same place. Even though the left kidney sits lower in the abdominal cavity, in some specimens the left renal vein enters the caudal vena cava above the right renal vein (Figure 5.15).

Author's Note: This is a convenient place to talk about developmental anomalies in these specimens. Different species of mammals naturally differ slightly in the association of some of their blood vessels and other organs. Some of these differences can be attributed to specific adaptations for different lifestyles (e.g., extent of cecum development in herbivores vs. carnivores) while others are probably the result of neutral mutations in genes controlling the embryonic development and differentiation of these structures. We even see differences in the vasculature of males and females of the same species for the latter reason. While these anomalies in the "plumbing" pose no real problems for the animals that possess them, it makes identification of corresponding structures more challenging for us! This phenomenon is compounded in minks by the extensive degree of inbreeding that occurs on mink ranches. This practice lowers genetic diversity and allows for an unusually high number of recessive alleles to accumulate in populations, further increasing the likelihood of developmental anomalies. As a result, many of the specimens you dissect will not look exactly like the photos we have provided. It is therefore imperative that you trace each vessel to its target organ/s to properly identify it. In many cases we have provided examples of the more "common" anomalies that we have encountered (with brief discussions), but you should be vigilant for other differences in your specimens.

In males the vessels draining blood from the testes, the **spermatic veins**, join the caudal vena cava below the junction of the renal veins. The two spermatic veins form a symmetrical, paired bifurcation from the vena cava (Figure 5.13B). In females the arrangement of the corresponding vessels, the **ovarian veins**, is somewhat different. While the right ovarian vein sends blood from the right ovary directly into the caudal vena cava, the left ovarian vein stretches cranially to join the left renal vein (Figure 5.13A and 5.15). Although unusual, this pattern seems to be consistent in female mink. Notice too, that this is not the case with the arterial supply to these organs. The **ovarian arteries** both branch directly off the aorta, although their branching is sometimes slightly offset. In males, the **spermatic arteries** also have a symmetrical, paired bifurcation from the aorta (Figure 5.13B). The remnant of a solitary vessel, the **caudal mesenteric artery**, should be seen branching off the ventral surface of the aorta caudal to the origin of the ovarian (or spermatic) arteries. This artery branches into the mesentery of the large intestines and supplies oxygenated blood to this region.

The **iliolumbar arteries and veins** represent the next major branches of the aorta and the caudal vena cava. Follow the aorta and caudal vena cava further caudally past the iliolumbar vessels. Here the aorta and vena cava split into two large arteries, the **right and left external**

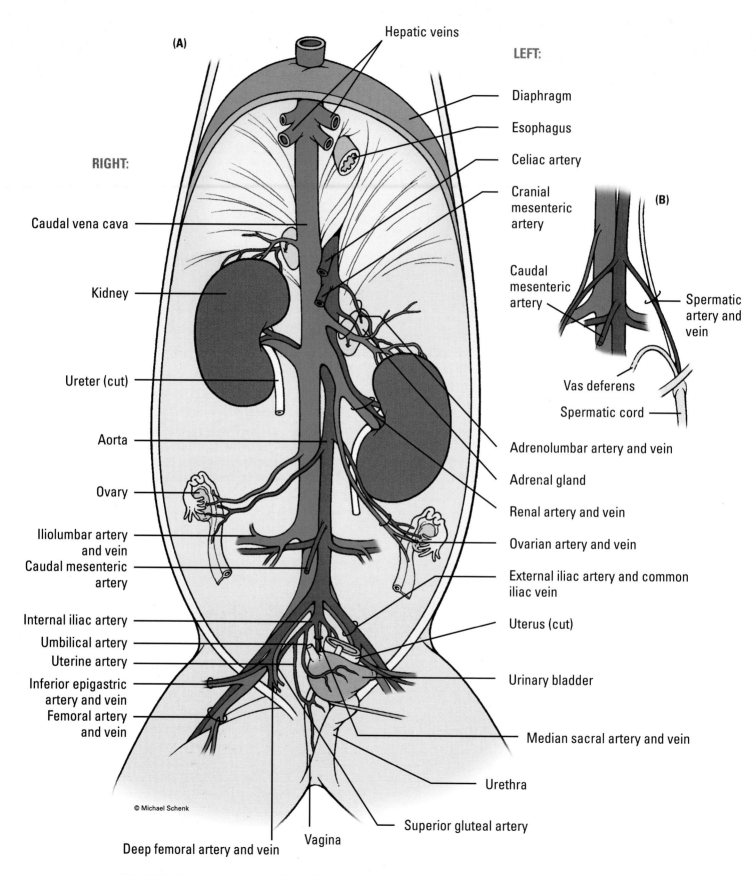

FIG. 5.13. *Illustration of arterial supply and venous return to organs in the abdominal cavity and the lower extremities in the female (A); male structures in inset (B).*

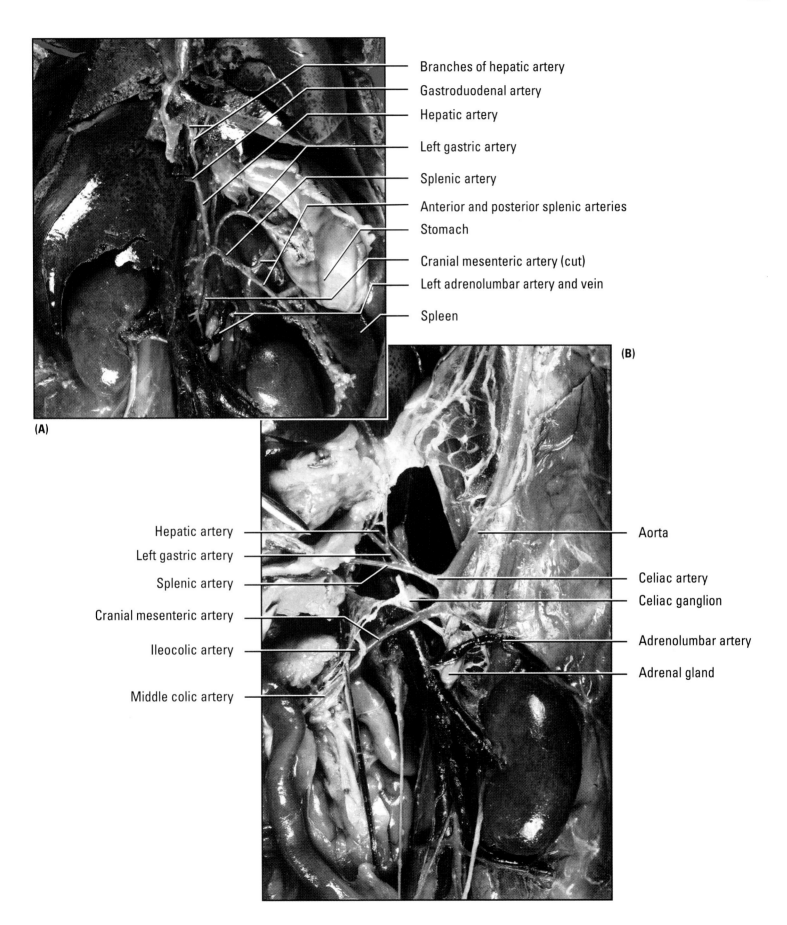

Branches of hepatic artery

Gastroduodenal artery

Hepatic artery

Left gastric artery

Splenic artery

Anterior and posterior splenic arteries

Stomach

Cranial mesenteric artery (cut)

Left adrenolumbar artery and vein

Spleen

(A)

(B)

Hepatic artery

Left gastric artery

Splenic artery

Cranial mesenteric artery

Ileocolic artery

Middle colic artery

Aorta

Celiac artery

Celiac ganglion

Adrenolumbar artery

Adrenal gland

FIG. 5.14. *Arteries of the upper abdominal region (A) and details of the celiac trunk (B).*

RIGHT: LEFT:

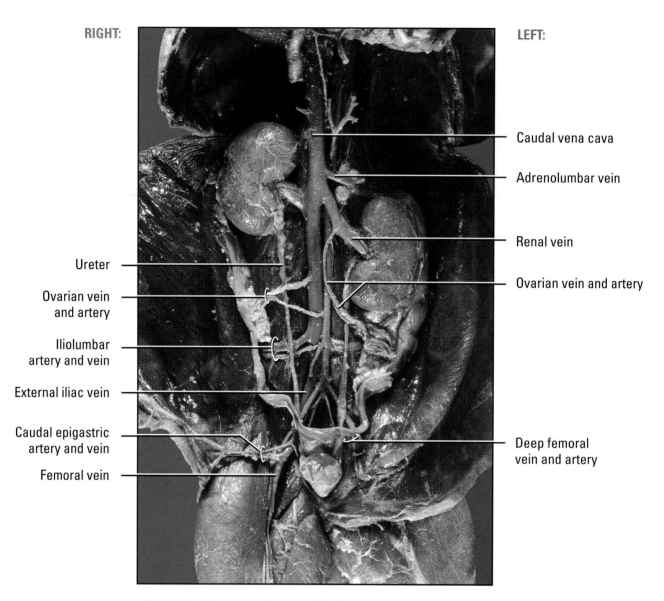

Caudal vena cava

Adrenolumbar vein

Renal vein

Ovarian vein and artery

Ureter

Ovarian vein
and artery

Iliolumbar
artery and vein

External iliac vein

Caudal epigastric
artery and vein   Deep femoral
                                                                          vein and artery
Femoral vein

▲ **FIG. 5.15.** *Arteries and veins of the abdominal region and hindlimbs.*

iliac arteries, and two large veins, the **right and left common iliac veins** (Figure 5.13 and 5.15). The external iliac arteries diverge into a number of smaller blood vessels supplying the hindlimbs and the common iliac veins represent a confluence of numerous vessels that collectively drain the hindlimbs. Another developmental anomaly can be seen in Figure 5.14. The male mink depicted in this figure has an unusually high bifurcation of the caudal vena cava into the common iliac veins. In this individual the common iliac veins have split off the caudal vena cava above the iliolumbar veins and run parallel to one another before diverging into the upper thigh of each hindlimb. Remember we said to keep your eyes open for differences!

As the external iliac arteries and common iliac veins continue along the hindlimb they each give off branches

known as the deep femoral arteries and veins, respectively. The **deep femoral arteries and veins** are the last sets of vessels that originate within the abdominal cavity. As the external iliac arteries and common iliac veins exit the body wall and continue along the hindlimb, their names change to the **femoral arteries and veins**. Shortly after they emerge from the abdominal cavity, the **inferior epigastric arteries and veins** branch off of them. The inferior epigastric arteries and veins are sometimes referred to as the caudal epigastric arteries and veins.

After the right and left external iliac arteries diverge from the aorta, the remaining aortic trunk quickly narrows and gives off **right and left internal iliac arteries** which split into numerous smaller arteries that supply blood to organs within the lower abdominal cavity. The **median sacral ar-**

tery is the first of these branches. In the female, the **umbilical artery** and the **uterine artery** are visible branching off the internal iliac arteries, with the umbilical artery leading to the urinary bladder and the uterine artery leading to the uterus (Figure 5.16). The umbilical artery is so named because it represents the remnant of the umbilical artery in the fetus that carried blood to the placenta during development. In the male, the umbilical artery is present, but the uterine artery is absent (Figure 5.17). Careful inspection of this area should also reveal the **middle hemorrhoidal artery** underneath the rectum. This small vessel supplies the urinary bladder, the rectum and some reproductive structures.

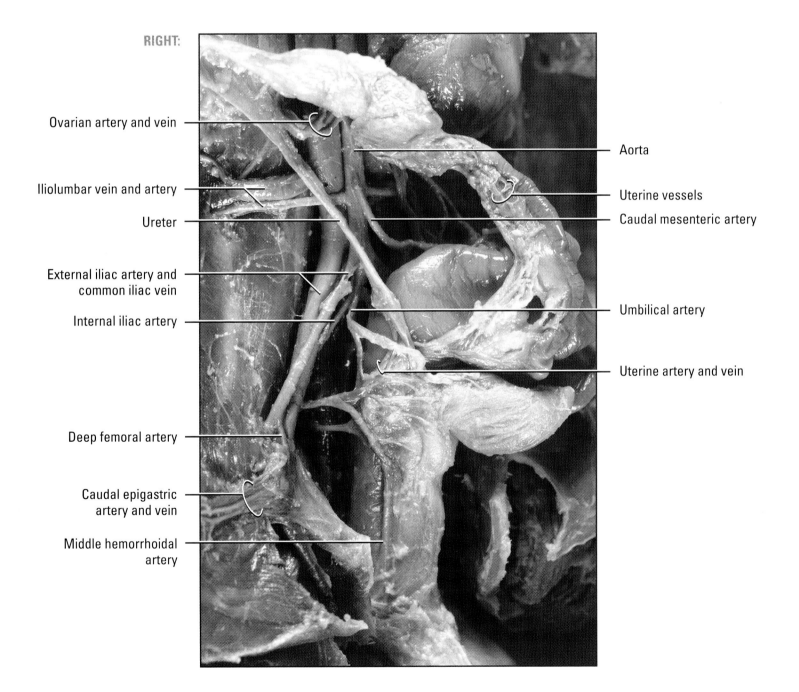

RIGHT:

Ovarian artery and vein

Iliolumbar vein and artery

Ureter

External iliac artery and common iliac vein

Internal iliac artery

Deep femoral artery

Caudal epigastric artery and vein

Middle hemorrhoidal artery

Aorta

Uterine vessels

Caudal mesenteric artery

Umbilical artery

Uterine artery and vein

▲ **FIG. 5.16.** *Genitovesicular arteries and veins in the female.*

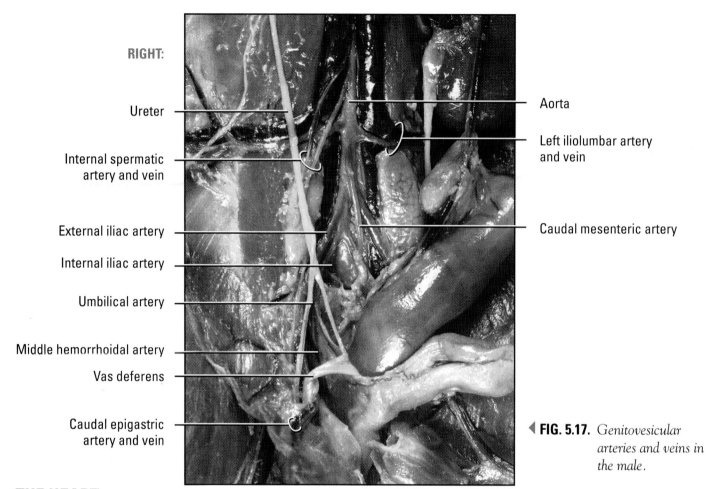

RIGHT:

Ureter

Internal spermatic
artery and vein

External iliac artery

Internal iliac artery

Umbilical artery

Middle hemorrhoidal artery

Vas deferens

Caudal epigastric
artery and vein

Aorta

Left iliolumbar artery
and vein

Caudal mesenteric artery

◀ **FIG. 5.17.** *Genitovesicular
arteries and veins in
the male.*

THE HEART

Due to the popularity of the sheep heart in many courses, the following section will contain photos of both the mink and sheep heart. Either heart will suffice as a model for studying the "typical" mammalian heart. The primary difference between the two will be reflected in the smaller size and slightly elongated, oval shape of the mink heart (Figure 5.18). If you are using a commercially prepared sheep heart you may skip the procedures in the following highlighted section for removing the mink heart from the body.

INSTRUCTION

If you plan to complete the dissection using the mink heart, carefully remove the heart from the thoracic cavity by cutting the (1) aorta, (2) pulmonary arteries, (3) cranial and caudal vena cavae and (4) pulmonary veins. Cut each vessel carefully and try to leave a significant portion of each vessel attached to the heart.

Author's Note: Throughout this chapter, we use the terms atrium and auricle to refer to different regions of the heart. The term auricle is used to describe the small, outer, flap-like region that covers a portion of the atrial chamber, while the term atrium is used to refer to the entire open space (or actual chamber) inside that collects the blood. The reason for this distinction is that part of each atrial chamber extends well beyond the boundaries of each flap-like auricle. This is evident when you view the interior of the heart.

Identify the four chambers of the mink (or sheep) heart. Caudally there are two large, thick-walled ventricles, the **right ventricle** and the **left ventricle** (Figure 5.18–5.19). These chambers pump blood out of the heart to the lungs and to the rest of the body, respectively. In the sheep heart, there is a superficial landmark separating these two chambers known as the **interventricular groove** that runs obliquely down the ventral surface of the heart toward the **apex**, but runs more longitudinally on the dorsal surface of the heart. Cranial to the ventricles and somewhat darker in color are the **right and left auricles**. Chambers within the right and left auricles receive blood from the body and the lungs, respectively, and pass it to the ventricles. Running along the surface of the heart itself are the small **coronary** arteries and **veins**. The coronary arteries supply blood to the heart muscle, ensuring that it too receives nutrients and oxygen to maintain an energy supply to support its continuous, methodical beating throughout the entire life of the animal (Figures 5.18C and 5.19D). In the mink, the coronary vessels are quite noticeable, but in the sheep they are typically buried under dense fat on the surface of the heart.

INSTRUCTION

You may need to clear away fat from the major arteries and veins originating from the heart. Use scissors to carefully snip off pieces of fat and other connective tissue until you have isolated the major vessels of the heart.

Notice remnants of the large veins entering the heart on the right side. These are the **cranial** and **caudal vena cavae** (Figures 5.18–5.19). They bring deoxygenated blood to the right atrium from the upper and lower portions of the body. On the dorsal surface of the heart, adjacent to the juncture of the vena cavae and the right atrium, there is a small sac-like region of the heart known as the **coronary sinus** (Figure 5.18B). This sinus is responsible for returning deoxygenated blood from the wall of the heart to the right atrium. The most visible artery from the ventral surface leaving the heart is the large **pulmonary artery** emanating from the right ventricle. This artery channels blood from the right ventricle through the right and left pulmonary arteries to the lungs. Also notice the large, thick-walled **aorta** leaving the heart from the cranial aspect of the left ventricle. The aorta and pulmonary artery are connected for a short distance by remnant tissue of the ductus arteriosus that diverted blood from the pulmonary artery to the aorta during fetal development. This band of solid connective tissue now joining these two vessels is known as the **ligamentum arteriosum**. In the sheep heart, the large **brachiocephalic artery** will also be visible as the first branch off the aorta. On the dorsal surface of the heart you should be able to identify the **pulmonary veins** leading back to the left auricle.

INSTRUCTION

To cut the sheep heart in half, you will need a large, sharp knife with a blade that is several inches longer than the width of the heart. Place the sheep heart (or mink heart) in a dissecting pan and make a longitudinal cut along the frontal plane of the heart (dividing it into roughly equal dorsal and ventral halves). You will need to use a "sawing" motion to cut through the heart. Be very precise in your motion so that you do not "rip" through the heart, but rather slice through it cleanly.

Notice that the atrial chambers extend well beyond the boundaries of each auricle (as mentioned earlier) and that the walls of the atria are much thinner than the walls of the ventricles. Since the ventricles are responsible for pumping blood much greater distances, they have evolved into heavily muscularized chambers capable of generating massive pressure to force blood out of the heart and through the body. Notice that inside the chambers of the heart there are valves to prevent blood from flowing backwards (Figures 5.18C, 5.19C and 5.19D). As blood enters the right atrium, it immediately flows into the right ventricle. Very little blood is actually *pumped* by the right atrium into the right ventricle. At the juncture of the right atrium and right ventricle there is a **tricuspid valve**. As the right ventricle contracts and pushes blood out to the lungs, some blood is forced back up against the tricuspid valve, slamming its leaflets shut and preventing retrograde flow into the right atrium. Upon entering the pulmonary trunk, the blood also passes through the **pulmonary semilunar valve**, which prevents backflow into the right ventricle as it relaxes and receives more blood from the right atrium. Fully oxygenated blood returns from the lungs into the left atrium via the pulmonary veins and then flows into the left ventricle through the **bicuspid** (or **mitral**) valve. Blood leaving the left ventricle into the aorta passes through the **aortic semilunar valve**, another valve to prevent backflow as this ventricle relaxes. The bicuspid and tricuspid valves are prevented from being pushed too far backward (a condition known as "prolapse") by small stringlike attachments of connective tissue called **chordae tendineae** which have small muscular attachments (**papillary muscles**) to the inner wall of the heart (Figure 5.18C and 5.19C).

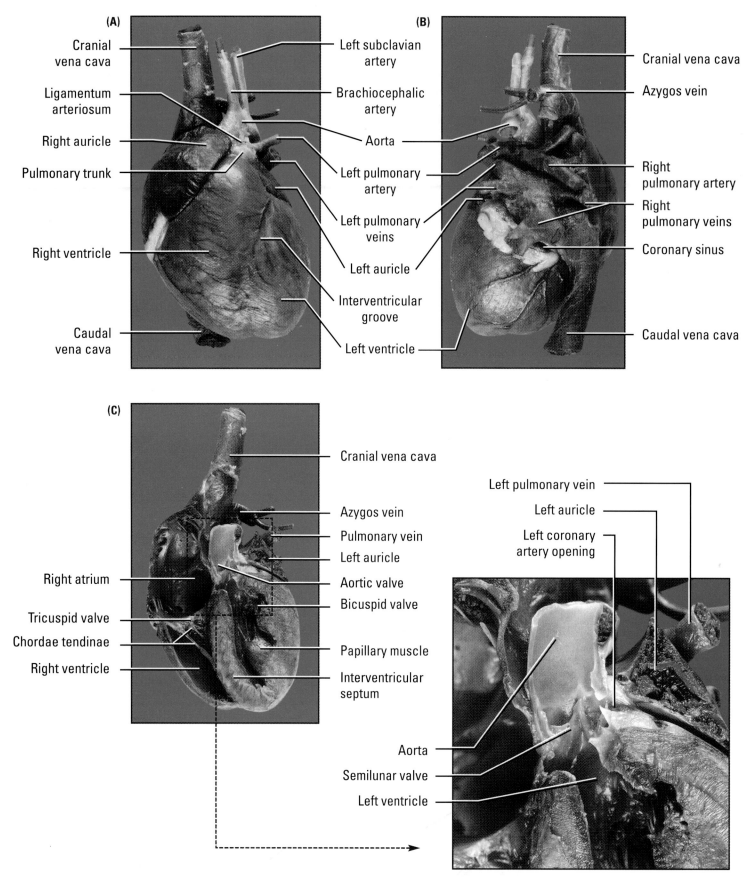

FIG. 5.18. *Dorsal view (A), ventral view (B) and interior view through frontal plain of the mink heart (C) with inset depicting section through coronary artery.*

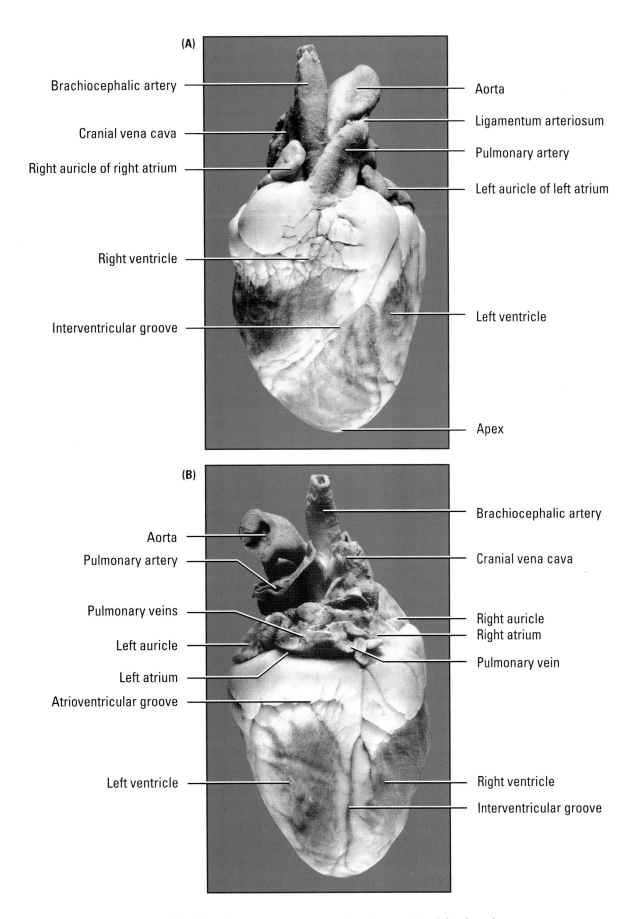

(A)

Brachiocephalic artery

Cranial vena cava

Right auricle of right atrium

Right ventricle

Interventricular groove

Aorta

Ligamentum arteriosum

Pulmonary artery

Left auricle of left atrium

Left ventricle

Apex

(B)

Aorta

Pulmonary artery

Pulmonary veins

Left auricle

Left atrium

Atrioventricular groove

Left ventricle

Brachiocephalic artery

Cranial vena cava

Right auricle
Right atrium

Pulmonary vein

Right ventricle

Interventricular groove

▲ **FIG. 5.19.** *Ventral view (A) and dorsal view (B) of the sheep heart.*

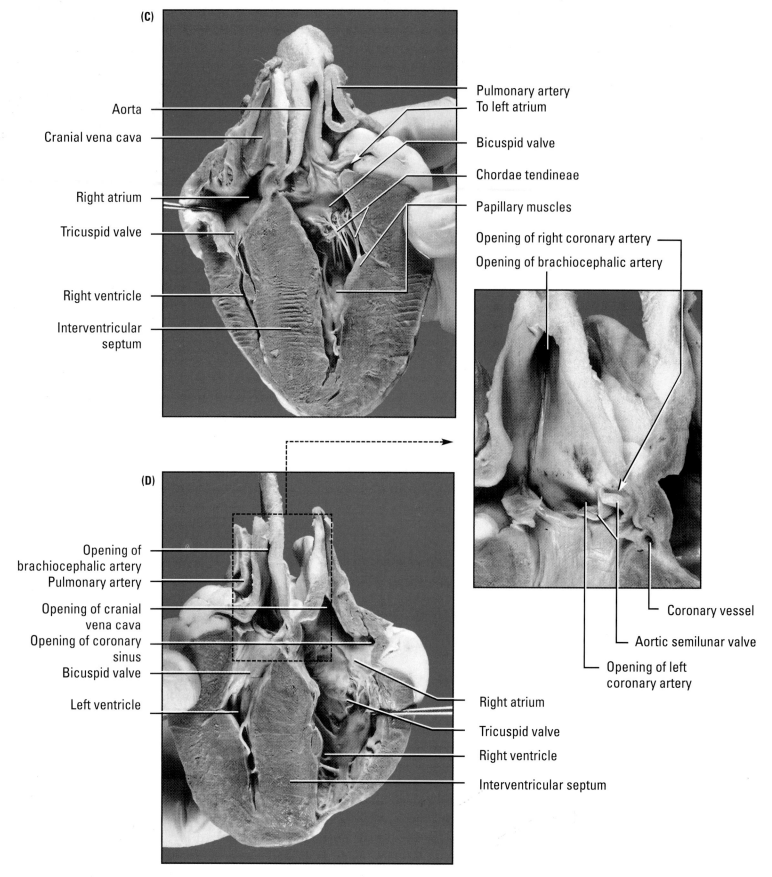

(C)

Aorta

Cranial vena cava

Right atrium

Tricuspid valve

Right ventricle

Interventricular
septum

Pulmonary artery
To left atrium

Bicuspid valve

Chordae tendineae

Papillary muscles

Opening of right coronary artery

Opening of brachiocephalic artery

(D)

Opening of
brachiocephalic artery
Pulmonary artery

Opening of cranial
vena cava
Opening of coronary
sinus
Bicuspid valve

Left ventricle

Coronary vessel

Aortic semilunar valve

Opening of left
coronary artery

Right atrium

Tricuspid valve

Right ventricle

Interventricular septum

▲ **FIG. 5.19.** *Dorsal half of frontal section* (C) *and ventral half of frontal section* (D) *of the sheep heart with inset depicting openings to coronary arteries.*

Respiratory System

6

LABORATORY OBJECTIVES

After completing this chapter, you should be able to:

1. Identify the major respiratory structures of the mink.

2. Discuss the function of all indicated structures.

3. Discuss the flow of oxygen and carbon dioxide through the respiratory system.

4. Identify the microanatomy of respiratory tissues.

The respiratory system of mammals is responsible for bringing a fresh supply of oxygen to the bloodstream and carrying off excess carbon dioxide. The anatomy of the respiratory tract is designed to humidify and warm the air while filtering out dust particles and germs. The lining of the nasal epithelium is covered with fine hairs that capture these foreign particles and prevent them from passing into the lungs where they may infect the body. Similarly, as air is exhaled it is cooled and dried, thus reducing the amount of heat and moisture that terrestrial animals lose through respiration.

INSTRUCTION

Using scissors, extend the midline incision (made earlier) by cutting cranially along the ventral midline of your mink from the top of the rib cage toward the chin. Be careful, many glands and organs lie just under the skin and may be damaged if you cut too deeply. Carefully tease away the surrounding tissue to expose the trachea.

THE THORACIC CAVITY

The **trachea** is a long tube reinforced with cartilaginous rings to prevent collapse as the mink inhales (Figures 6.1–6.2). This tube leads from the nasopharynx (identified earlier) through the larynx ("voice box") and into the lungs. Locate the **larynx**. It should appear as an enlarged, oval-shaped protrusion toward the cranial end of the trachea. The larynx allows mammals to have a vast repertoire of vocalizations ranging from ultrasonic squeaks and chirps (in bats) and guttural barks or grunts (in dogs and pigs) to the highly complex sounds of human speech. The pitch of these vocalizations is controlled by muscles attached to the larynx which contract and relax, altering the shape of the voice box, thus changing the sounds that it produces. Follow the trachea caudally toward the lungs. Notice where it splits into the two **bronchi** (Figures 6.2–6.3). These lead into the **left** and **right lung**. Notice that the right lung has four lobes, while the left lung has two. (In humans, the right lung has three lobes, while the left has two.) Identify the **right cranial lobe, right medial lobe, right caudal lobe** and **accessory lobe**. On the left side of the mink, locate the **left cranial lobe** and **left caudal lobe**. The individual lobes are distinguished by the internal divisions of bronchi and not by the apparent superficial divisions. Just caudal to the lungs you should be able to see a thin muscular sheet of tissue, the **diaphragm**.

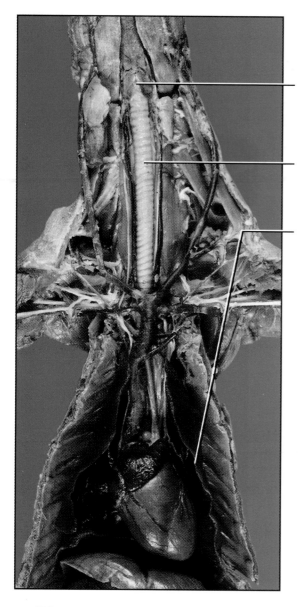

▲ **FIG. 6.1.** *Respiratory system of mink (lungs in thoracic cavity).*

Larynx

Trachea

Lungs in thoracic cavity

This structure (unique to mammals) allows the thoracic cavity to expand and compress, drawing in fresh air with each expansion (as the diaphragm contracts) and expelling stale air with each compression (as the diaphragm relaxes).

Inside the lungs, the bronchi are further divided into several branches called **bronchioles** (Figure 6.3). These bronchioles branch into smaller and smaller tubules, eventually terminating in open sacs called **alveoli**. These alveoli are comprised of thin epithelial tissue and are surrounded by capillary networks. It is here where oxygen is picked up by the bloodstream and carbon dioxide is released into the lungs to be expelled from the body through exhalation.

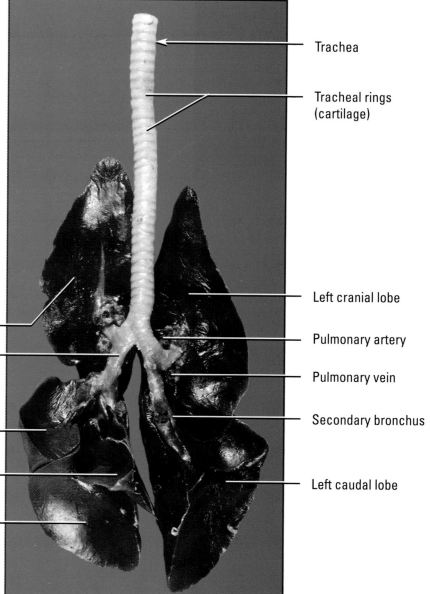

Trachea

Tracheal rings (cartilage)

Left cranial lobe

Pulmonary artery

Pulmonary vein

Secondary bronchus

Left caudal lobe

Right cranial lobe

Primary bronchus

Right medial lobe

Accessory lobe

Right caudal lobe

FIG. 6.2. *Ventral view of lungs isolated from* ▶ *body with trachea attached.*

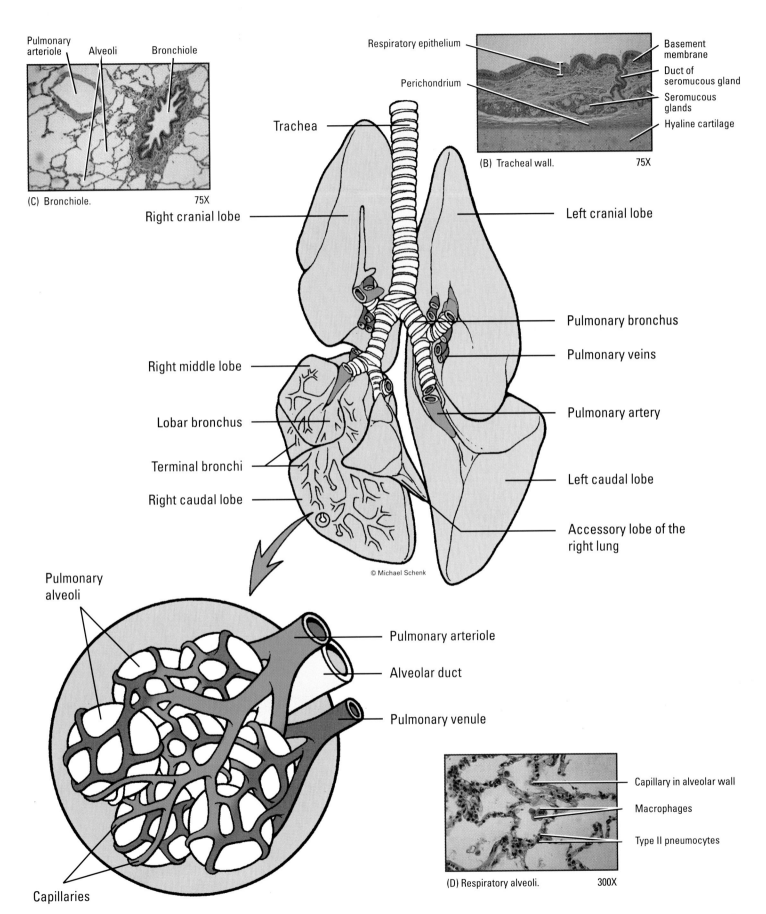

Pulmonary arteriole
Alveoli
Bronchiole

(C) Bronchiole.   75X

Respiratory epithelium
Basement membrane
Perichondrium
Duct of seromucous gland
Seromucous glands
Hyaline cartilage

(B) Tracheal wall.   75X

Trachea

Right cranial lobe
Left cranial lobe

Right middle lobe
Pulmonary bronchus
Pulmonary veins

Lobar bronchus
Pulmonary artery

Terminal bronchi

Right caudal lobe
Left caudal lobe

Accessory lobe of the right lung

© Michael Schenk

Pulmonary alveoli

Pulmonary arteriole
Alveolar duct
Pulmonary venule

Capillaries

Capillary in alveolar wall
Macrophages
Type II pneumocytes

(D) Respiratory alveoli.   300X

FIG. 6.3. *Illustration of lungs showing alveolar sacs; histology photographs of (B) tracheal wall, (C) bronchiole and (D) alveoli.*

THE ORAL CAVITY

As the mink inhales, air is taken in through the external **nares** and passes through the **nasopharynx**. At this point, the **glottis** is "open," with the **epiglottis** permitting air flow through the **larynx** into the **trachea** (Figure 6.4A). However, when the mink swallows, food passes through the oral cavity (on the ventral side of the hard and soft palates) and is prevented from entering the respiratory tract by the action of the epiglottis closing to cover the entrance to the glottis (Figure 6.4B). In the evolution of vertebrates, the advent of the complete secondary palate (the continuous hard and soft palate) was a major advancement. Animals could now eat with no interruption in respiratory capability, since the complete secondary palate effectively keeps the food passageway and airway separated. Reptiles which lack a complete secondary palate must pause while eating, take a few deep breaths, and then resume swallowing their food. Overcoming this constraint was one of many developments which contributed to mammals' ability to maintain a high metabolic rate and become endothermic. Endothermy is extremely costly and requires a high metabolism which obligates an animal to consume large quantities of nutrients without interruption.

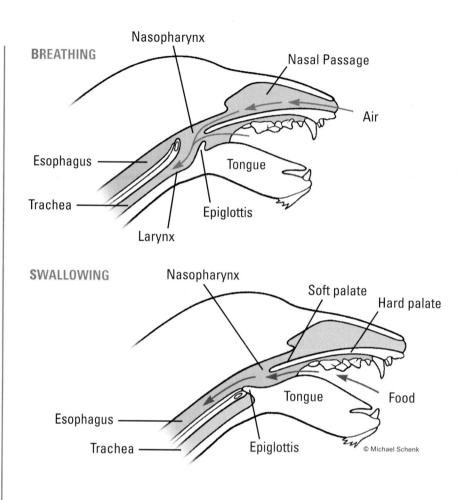

FIG. 6.4. *Illustrations depicting mechanisms of breathing (A) and swallowing (B) in the mink.*

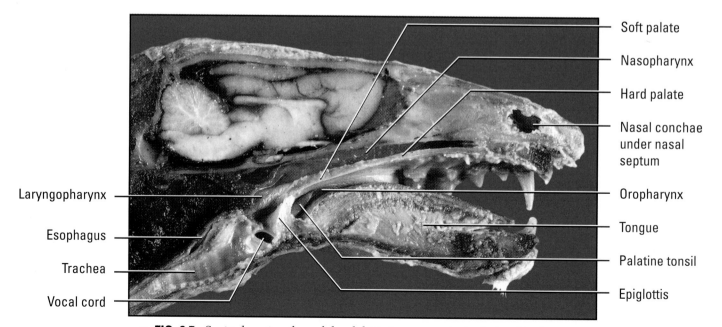

FIG. 6.5. *Sagittal section through head depicting anatomical relationships between oral and nasal cavities and associated structures.*

CHAPTER 7

Reproductive and Excretory Systems

LABORATORY OBJECTIVES

After completing this chapter, you should be able to:

1. Identify the major excretory structures of the mink.

2. Identify the major reproductive structures of both male and female minks.

3. Discuss the function of all indicated structures.

4. Identify the microanatomy of the excretory and reproductive organs.

REPRODUCTIVE SYSTEM

The reproductive system is responsible for producing **gametes** that will ultimately fuse with the corresponding gamete of the opposite sex. Because successful reproduction depends solely upon an individual's ability to pass its genes on to the next generation, reproductive systems within species have evolved highly complex features and mechanisms that increase the chances of fertilization and successful embryonic development. In addition to reproduction, the organs of gametogenesis (testes and ovaries) are responsible for producing many of the hormones associated with the development and maturation of primary and secondary sexual characteristics and for driving the repertoire of sexual behaviors indicative of a particular species. The hormone products of these organs will be discussed in depth in Chapter 9.

INSTRUCTION

Using a blunt probe, extend the incision made earlier caudally along the ventral midline of the lower abdominal region toward the anus. If you have a male mink, continue on with the next section. If you have a female mink, skip ahead to the section entitled "Female Reproductive System." **However, regardless of the sex of your mink, you are expected to be familiar with the structures of each sex, so work closely with another group that has a mink of the opposite sex.** Remember, female minks are not likely to be plentiful in your shipment, since all but a few are kept for breeding purposes. Check to see if your instructor has a female dissected as a demonstration for the class.

Male Reproductive System

The **scrotal sacs** of the male house the **testes**, small bean-shaped structures where sperm production occurs. These sacs will be missing from your specimen; however one or both of the testes should still be present. Your first task in dissecting the male reproductive system is to locate the spermatic cords which leave the scrotum and enter the abdominal wall of the mink (Figures 7.1–7.2). Despite the absence of the scrotal sacs, each testis should still be enclosed within a **cremasteric pouch**. At the cranial end of the cremasteric pouch, a narrow tube should be evident. This is the **spermatic cord** which contains the vas deferens, the spermatic artery and vein, lymphatic vessels and numerous nerves. The testes will be located within the cremasteric pouch.

INSTRUCTION

Carefully make a slit in the cremasteric pouch and peel it open, using scissors if necessary. Leave the testis attached to the spermatic cord, but separate it from the tissue of the cremasteric pouch.

Cupped around the side of each testis is a highly-coiled system of tubules known as the **epididymis** (Figure 7.1A). Sperm are produced within the **seminiferous tubules** of the testes and are stored along the length of the epididymis, with newly-produced sperm located at the head of the epididymis and "older" sperm located toward the tail of the epididymis. Notice that the convolutions of the epididymis get larger and begin to straighten out as this continuous tube progresses from the head toward the tail of the epididymis. Upon ejaculation, sperm leave the epididymis and travel through the **vas deferens** toward the **urethra** (Table 7.1). Trace along the length of the spermatic cord to see the path sperm travel as they move out of the epididymis through the vas deferens (which loops around the ureter) toward the prostate region. Notice that there is an opening in the abdominal wall (the **inguinal canal**) through which the spermatic cord passes from the scrotum into the abdominal cavity. Now direct your attention to the penis. The first thing you may notice about the penis of the mink, other than its disproportionate length, is that it is enclosed in a sheath and held along the ventral wall of the abdomen. Humans have no such sheath; rather the penis hangs freely.

INSTRUCTION

Make a slit in the distal end of the sheath housing the penis and continue the incision away from the tip of the penis. To completely uncover all of the reproductive structures, including many of the accessory glands of this region, you may wish to cut longitudinally through the pubic symphysis with a scalpel. Be sure to cut carefully and start your incision to one side of the median plane of the pelvis to avoid actually cutting through the urethra or other underlying structures. It is preferable to only partially cut through the symphysis and then apply downward (lateral) pressure to each of the hindlimbs to complete the separation.

Careful dissection of this area may reveal several accessory glands along this route. The most obvious structure in this area is the large, white **prostate gland** (Figures 7.1–7.3). This organ is located at the juncture of the vas deferentia (= plural of vas deferens) and the urethra. You may be able to identify **seminal vesicles**. The **bulbourethral glands** lie caudally, on either side of the urethra near the **crus** of the penis (Figure 7.3A). Together, these glands contribute fluid to the sperm, over 60% of the total volume of the semen. This fluid is thick and contains mucus (to prevent the sperm from drying out) and large amounts of fructose (to provide energy for the sperm). In addition, the semen is highly basic to neutralize the acidic environment of the vagina and increase the chances of survival for the sperm. The semen passes through the **urethra** and into the **penis** from which it will be ejaculated. The proximal portion of the penis is comprised internally of the **corpus spongiosum** and two **corpus cavernosa** (singular = corpus cavernosum), three columns of highly vascularized erectile tissue that contain large sinuses to accommodate the corresponding increase in blood flow to the penis during erection. The distal portion of the penis is comprised of the **glans penis** and the **prepuce** (the pocket of skin that encloses the glans penis). As you may remember from Chapter 2, the penis of the mink also contains a bone (os penis) that assists in maintaining erection.

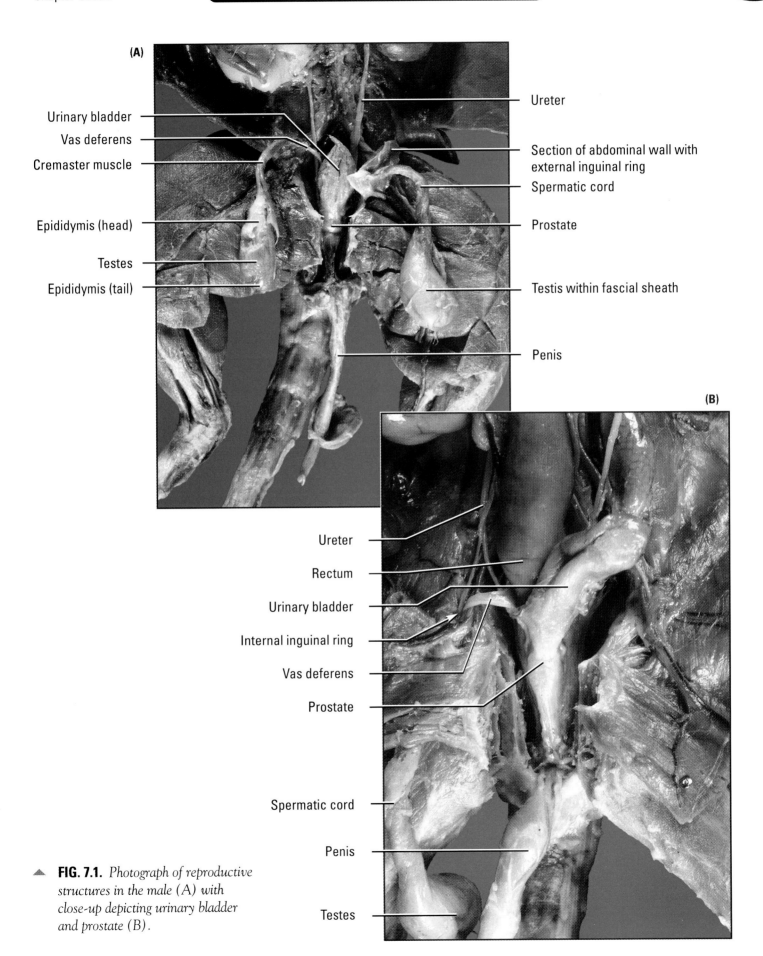

(A)

Urinary bladder

Vas deferens

Cremaster muscle

Epididymis (head)

Testes

Epididymis (tail)

Ureter

Section of abdominal wall with external inguinal ring

Spermatic cord

Prostate

Testis within fascial sheath

Penis

(B)

Ureter

Rectum

Urinary bladder

Internal inguinal ring

Vas deferens

Prostate

Spermatic cord

Penis

Testes

▲ **FIG. 7.1.** *Photograph of reproductive structures in the male (A) with close-up depicting urinary bladder and prostate (B).*

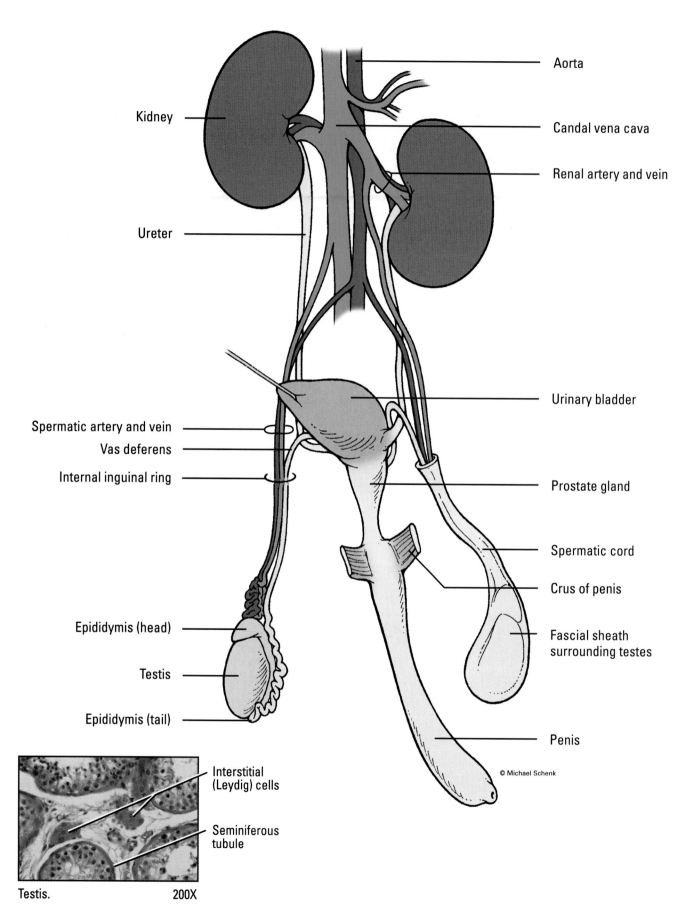

Aorta

Kidney

Candal vena cava

Renal artery and vein

Ureter

Urinary bladder

Spermatic artery and vein

Vas deferens

Internal inguinal ring

Prostate gland

Spermatic cord

Crus of penis

Epididymis (head)

Fascial sheath surrounding testes

Testis

Epididymis (tail)

Penis

© Michael Schenk

Interstitial (Leydig) cells

Seminiferous tubule

Testis.   200X

▲ **FIG. 7.2.** *Schematic illustration of male genitalia with histology photograph of testis; digestive tract omitted for clarity.*

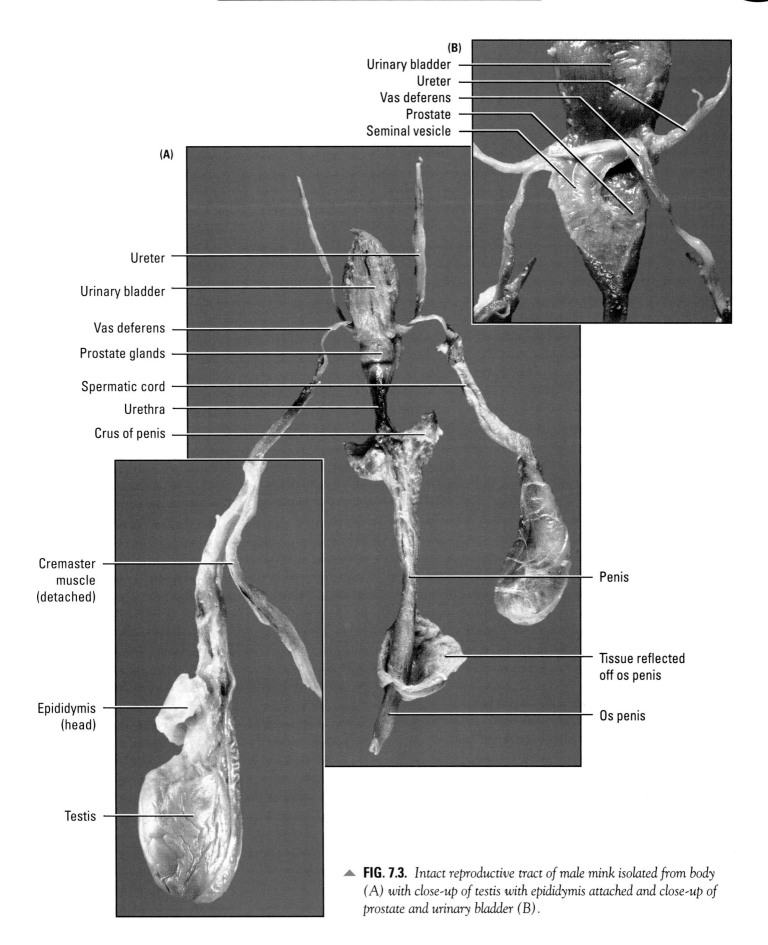

(B)
Urinary bladder
Ureter
Vas deferens
Prostate
Seminal vesicle

(A)

Ureter

Urinary bladder

Vas deferens

Prostate glands

Spermatic cord

Urethra

Crus of penis

Cremaster
muscle
(detached)

Epididymis
(head)

Testis

Penis

Tissue reflected
off os penis

Os penis

▲ **FIG. 7.3.** *Intact reproductive tract of male mink isolated from body (A) with close-up of testis with epididymis attached and close-up of prostate and urinary bladder (B).*

Female Reproductive System

The paired female gonads are called **ovaries** (Figures 7.4–7.5). They are located in the abdominal region caudal to the kidneys and can be identified by their small, round appearance. The ovaries are anchored to the dorsal wall of the abdominal cavity cranially by **suspensory ovarian ligaments**. Smaller, inconspicuous **ovarian ligaments** connect the ovaries to the cranial portions of each uterine horn. Attached to each ovary is a coiled oviduct. The **oviduct** receives the mature oocyte (egg) when it is released from the ovary at the time of ovulation. There is no actual physical connection between the oviductal opening and the ovary. Small finger-like projections of the oviduct, **fimbriae**, generate movements that sweep the egg into the oviduct. The epithelial lining of the oviduct is ciliated and creates a current that propels the egg along the length of the oviduct toward the horn of the uterus. Fertilization typically occurs in the upper third of the oviduct, but implantation of the embryos occurs further along in the uterus. In minks, the uterus is divided into two **uterine horns**, where embryonic development of the fetuses occurs, and a small **body of the uterus**, where the two uterine horns converge on the cervix (Figures 7.6 and 7.7). In humans, the uterine horns (known as fallopian tubes) are quite reduced, since the zygote implants in the body of the uterus, where embryonic development occurs. Due to larger litter sizes of 2–6 offspring (occasionally up to 10), the female mink requires a much larger area for young to develop, and the extensive size of the two uterine horns accommodates this need.

INSTRUCTION

As with the male, to completely uncover all of the reproductive structures, you may wish to cut longitudinally through the pubic symphysis with a scalpel. Be sure to cut carefully and start your incision slightly to one side of the median plane of the pelvis to avoid actually cutting through the uterus, urethra or other underlying structures. It is preferable to only partially cut through the symphysis and then apply downward (lateral) pressure to each of the hindlimbs to complete the separation. Use a teasing needle to carefully separate the fascia from the body of the uterus and the urethra to distinguish these structures and reveal the cervix and vaginal area. Use Figure 7.5 as a guide for this dissection.

The body of the uterus extends caudally to the cervix. Locate the juncture of the cervix and the vagina. The **cervix** is a constriction of semi-cartilaginous tissue, while the **vagina** extends caudally from this constriction. The vagina is joined by the urethra and the two converge into a common chamber called the **urogenital sinus** (since it handles products of both the urinary and reproductive systems). The urogenital sinus opens to the outside of the body through the **vestibule** (sometimes called the vaginal vestibule). Fleshy folds of skin are visible along the margins of the vestibule. These folds of skin are homologous to the labia in human females. A (very) small **clitoris** may be visible resting in a shallow depression along the mid-ventral line of the urogenital sinus. As a homologue to the male penis, this structure plays a similar role in sexual sensation and sends information about sexual stimulation to the brain. The entire region consisting of the labia, clitoris and vestibule are collectively referred to as the **vulva** (Table 7.1).

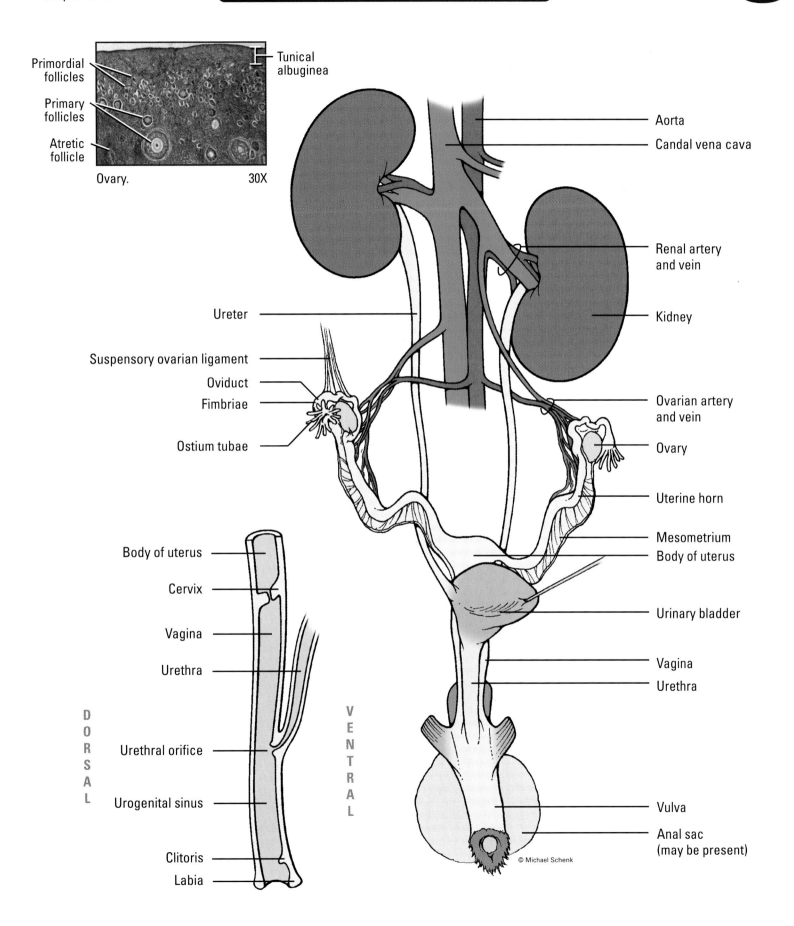

Primordial follicles

Primary follicles

Atretic follicle

Tunical albuginea

Ovary.

30X

Aorta

Candal vena cava

Renal artery and vein

Kidney

Ureter

Suspensory ovarian ligament

Oviduct

Fimbriae

Ostium tubae

Ovarian artery and vein

Ovary

Uterine horn

Mesometrium

Body of uterus

Body of uterus

Cervix

Vagina

Urethra

Urinary bladder

Vagina

Urethra

Urethral orifice

Urogenital sinus

Vulva

Anal sac (may be present)

Clitoris

Labia

DORSAL

VENTRAL

© Michael Schenk

▲ **FIG. 7.4.** *Illustration of female reproductive system with histology photograph of ovary.*

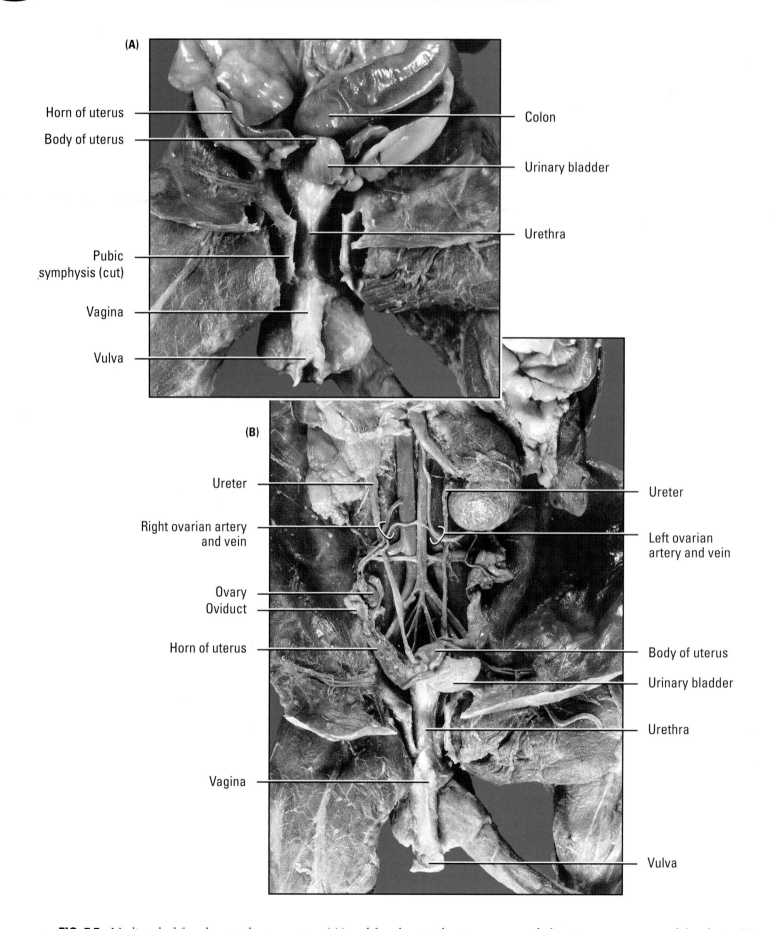

(A)

Horn of uterus

Body of uterus

Pubic symphysis (cut)

Vagina

Vulva

Colon

Urinary bladder

Urethra

(B)

Ureter

Right ovarian artery and vein

Ovary

Oviduct

Horn of uterus

Vagina

Ureter

Left ovarian artery and vein

Body of uterus

Urinary bladder

Urethra

Vulva

FIG. 7.5. *Undisturbed female reproductive system (A) and female reproductive system with digestive system removed for clarity (B).*

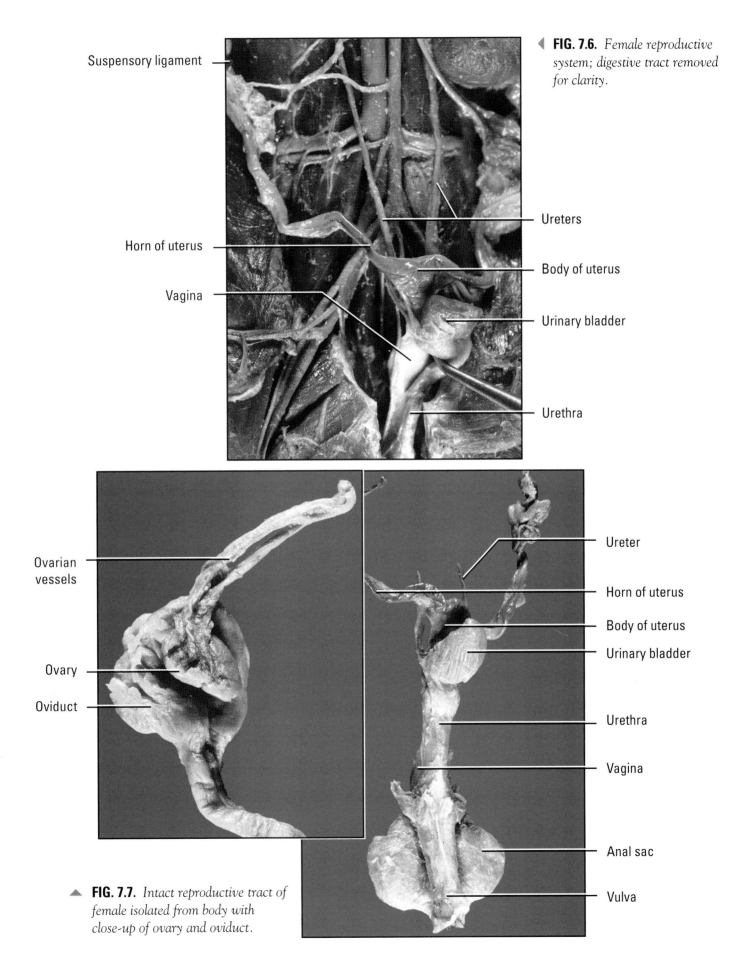

Suspensory ligament

Horn of uterus

Vagina

Ureters

Body of uterus

Urinary bladder

Urethra

◀ **FIG. 7.6.** *Female reproductive system; digestive tract removed for clarity.*

Ovarian vessels

Ovary

Oviduct

Ureter

Horn of uterus

Body of uterus

Urinary bladder

Urethra

Vagina

Anal sac

Vulva

▲ **FIG. 7.7.** *Intact reproductive tract of female isolated from body with close-up of ovary and oviduct.*

TABLE 7.1. *Male and female reproductive structures and their functions. Corresponding homologous structures in the two sexes are placed in the same row.*

MALE STRUCTURE	FUNCTION	FEMALE STRUCTURE	FUNCTION
Scrotal sacs	House testes	Vulva (labia)	Covers opening to vagina
Gubernaculum	Serves as cord for testes to follow on their embryonic descent into scrotum	Ovarian ligaments	Connect ovaries to uterine horns
Testis	Produces sperm	Ovary	Produces eggs
Epididymis*	Stores sperm	Oviduct*	Receives egg at ovulation; site of fertilization
Vas deferens*	Transports sperm to urethra	Uterine horns* (and body)	Site of implantation and embryonic development
Urethra	Receives seminal secretions from accessory glands	Urethra	Drains excretory products from urinary bladder *(no actual reproductive function)*
		Urogenital sinus (also homologous to distal portion of urethra in male)	Common chamber for the release of urinary products and acquisition of sperm
Penis	Deposits semen in female reproductive tract	Clitoris	Plays a role in sexual sensation and stimulation
Prostate gland	Contributes seminal fluid that may aid in neutralization of acidity of vagina	Vagina	Receives penis during copulation; serves as part of birth canal
Bulbourethral glands	Contribute seminal fluid that aids in neutralization of acidity of vagina		
Seminal vesicles	Contribute seminal fluid containing nutrients for sperm, and hormones to stimulate uterine contractions		

* *These structures are technically not homologous because they develop from separate embryonic tubes.*

EXCRETORY SYSTEM

The excretory system is responsible for eliminating the metabolic wastes that the body produces from cellular respiration and maintaining a homeostatic balance between the levels of fluids, electrolytes, sugars, hormones and proteins in the body. Remember, excretion is an entirely different process from that which expels undigested foodstuffs through the anus! Excretion and egestion (or defecation) are different processes, handled by completely different systems in vertebrates.

The **kidneys** are large, bean-shaped organs that lie along the dorsal surface of the abdominal cavity on either side of the spine (Figure 7.8). Notice how they are offset in the mink, with the right kidney lying more cranially than the left kidney. You have already seen the large **renal arteries** and **renal veins** that carry blood into and out of the kidneys (Figure 7.9). These organs filter blood from the circulatory system, removing the metabolic waste products produced in the tissues of the body during cellular respiration. Their major function is to concentrate these toxins and eliminate them from the body while conserving water, salts and other compounds that the body needs. In humans, the kidneys filter from 1100 to 2000 liters of blood each day! From this tremendous volume of blood only about 1.5 liters of urine is actually produced. The other 99.9% is reabsorbed into the bloodstream through a highly efficient system of semi-permeable tubules and concentration gradients in and around the **nephrons** of the kidney. The urine is concentrated in the kidneys and passes down each **ureter**, tubes lined with smooth muscle that transport the urine toward the **urinary bladder**. The urinary bladder is also a muscular reservoir that can expand to many times its "relaxed" size to accommodate large volumes of urine.

When relaxed, the inner walls of the bladder appear folded, resembling the rugae of the stomach lining. Eventually, the stored urine is eliminated through the **urethra**.

The kidney is comprised of three major regions internally. The outer region, the **cortex**, the middle region, the **medulla**, and the inner-most region, the **renal pelvis**. Locate these regions on the frontal section of the kidney you bisected (Figure 7.10). Notice how the renal pelvis drains into the ureter. The renal pelvis collects the waste that is filtered from the blood. The functional unit of the mammalian kidney is called the **nephron**. The nephron is comprised of many substructures which together filter nitrogenous wastes from the blood while conserving valuable sugars, electrolytes and water. Blood enters each nephron through an **afferent arteriole** that forms a capillary bed known as the **glomerulus**. Here, blood pressure forces water, urea, salts and other small soluble compounds from the blood into the epithelial lining of **Bowman's capsule**. Blood fluid that is not filtered out travels through an **efferent arteriole** to a capillary bed surrounding the convoluted tubules known as the **peritubular arteries**. Bowman's capsule receives the fluid and transports it along a series of **proximal convoluted tubules**, down the **loop of Henle** and through another series of **distal convoluted tubules**. During this stage of the filtration process, sodium, potassium and chloride ions as well as water are reabsorbed into the bloodstream. This process produces a highly concentrated urine that passes into a **collecting duct**. Many nephrons converge at the collecting ducts which drain the kidney. The urine passes from the kidney into the **ureter** and on to the **urinary bladder** for storage. Later, the urine will be eliminated from the mink through the **urethra** (Table 7.2).

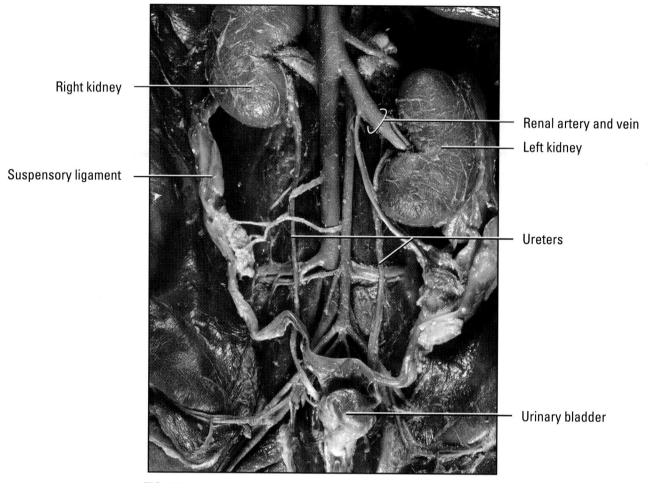

Right kidney

Suspensory ligament

Renal artery and vein

Left kidney

Ureters

Urinary bladder

FIG. 7.8. *Excretory system of mink; digestive tract removed for clarity.*

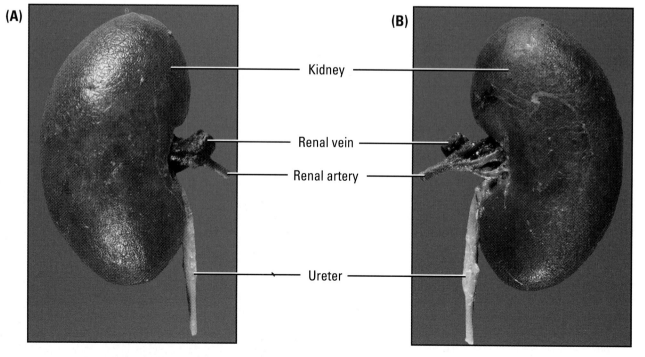

(A)

(B)

Kidney

Renal vein

Renal artery

Ureter

FIG. 7.9. *Right kidney of the mink—ventral view (A) and dorsal view (B).*

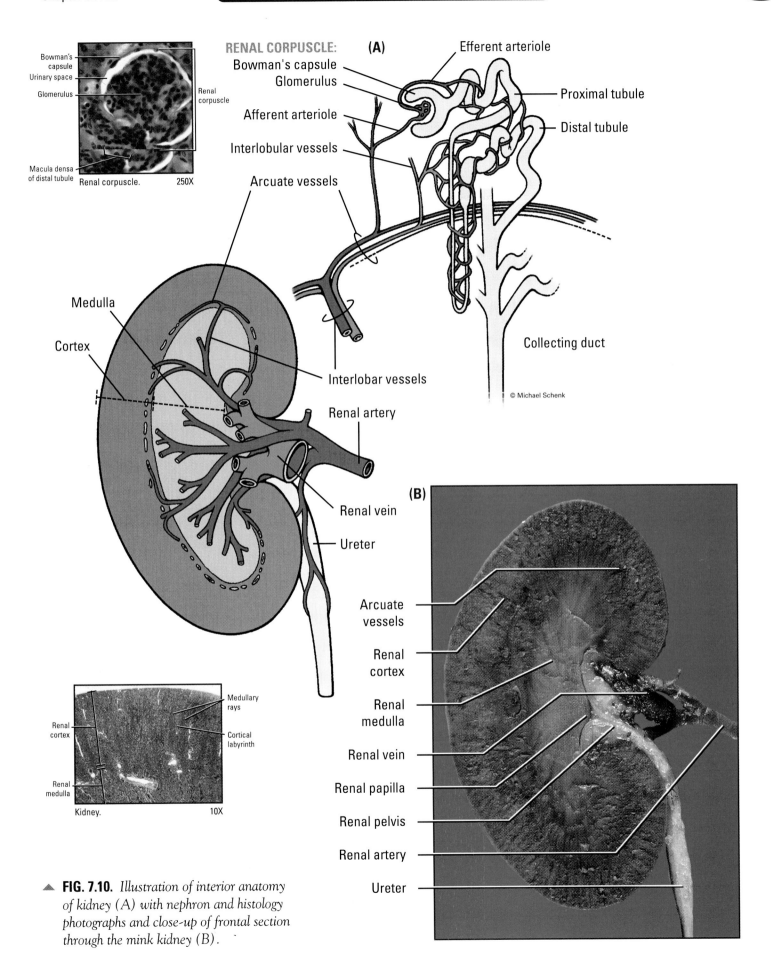

FIG. 7.10. *Illustration of interior anatomy of kidney (A) with nephron and histology photographs and close-up of frontal section through the mink kidney (B).*

TABLE 7.2. *Subunits of the mammalian kidney and urinary system and their functions.*

ORGAN STRUCTURE	FUNCTION
Renal artery	Supplies blood to the kidney
Renal vein	Transports filtered blood away from kidney to vena cava
Afferent arteriole	Brings blood to each nephron to be filtered
Efferent arteriole	Carries unfiltered portion of blood away from glomerulus to the capillary beds surrounding convoluted tubules and loop of Henle
Glomerulus	Capillary bed that forces fluid containing salts, glucose, vitamins and nitrogenous wastes out of the bloodstream
Bowman's capsule	Epithelial layer surrounding glomerulus that receives filtrate from the glomerulus
Proximal convoluted tubules	Series of tubules that selectively remove sodium chloride, potassium, water and other nutrients from the nephron and return them to the bloodstream
Peritubular arteries	Capillary bed surrounding the convoluted tubules
Loop of Henle	Long extension of the nephron tubule that descends into the medulla of the kidney forming a concentration gradient which removes more water and sodium chloride, and produces a highly-concentrated urine
Distal convoluted tubules	Series of tubules that selectively remove more water and sodium chloride, but absorb potassium
Collecting ducts	Several nephrons converge on a single collecting duct, which further concentrates urine while passing it along to the ureter
Ureter	Transports urine to the urinary bladder
Urinary bladder	Stores urine

Nervous System

LABORATORY OBJECTIVES

After completing this chapter, you should be able to:

1. Describe the organization of the vertebrate brain and spinal cord.

2. Identify the origins and functions of the twelve cranial nerves.

3. Identify the major nerves of the brachial plexus.

4. Identify the major structures associated with the sheep eye and describe their roles in vision.

The nervous system serves as the reconnaissance division of the body—receiving physical stimuli from the environment, converting it into electrical impulses, processing the information and effecting behavioral or physiological changes in response to the stimuli. The nervous system is divided into two main regions: the central nervous system (CNS), composed of the brain and spinal cord, and the peripheral nervous system (PNS), which includes the cranial nerves and spinal nerves emanating from the brain and spinal cord, respectively. The nerves of the PNS receive external stimuli (through sensory neurons) and produce motions in the muscles (through motor neurons). The brain and spinal cord are the sites of integration of the information picked up by the sensory neurons. These individual nerve cells are networked together to produce a highly complex, intricately organized system for communication and information transfer. You will dissect a large portion of the CNS and two specialized regions of the PNS (the brachial plexus and the eye).

Rather than dissecting the brain of your mink (which is *extremely* difficult and time consuming), we suggest you use a commercially prepared sheep brain. Since this option is generally the preferred route that most institutions take, the photos and illustrations that accompany this section of the manual will depict only the sheep brain.

THE BRAIN

The first apparent feature of the brain is its convoluted surface (Figures 8.1–8.3). The ridges you see are called **gyri** (singular = gyrus) and the grooves between the ridges are known as **sulci** (singular = sulcus). Because of this feature, the mammalian brain is referred to as **gyrencephalic**, as opposed to **lissencephalic** which refers to a brain that has a smooth outer surface. The advantage of a highly-convoluted brain surface is the increase in total cortical area that can be accommodated in the same sized cranial space; thus a more complex brain, capable of more complex behaviors and thought processes, is possible. The most prominent sulcus is the **longitudinal** (or **sagittal**) **fissure** that divides the two hemispheres of the cerebrum into **left and right hemispheres**. Internally the two hemispheres are separated by the **corpus callosum** (not visible externally), which forms the floor of the longitudinal fissure on the exterior surface of the brain (Figure 8.4). If a sagittal section through the brain is available to view, you will easily be able to locate the corpus callosum. The **cerebrum**, the largest portion of the brain, functions in the interpretation of sensory impulses and the coordination of

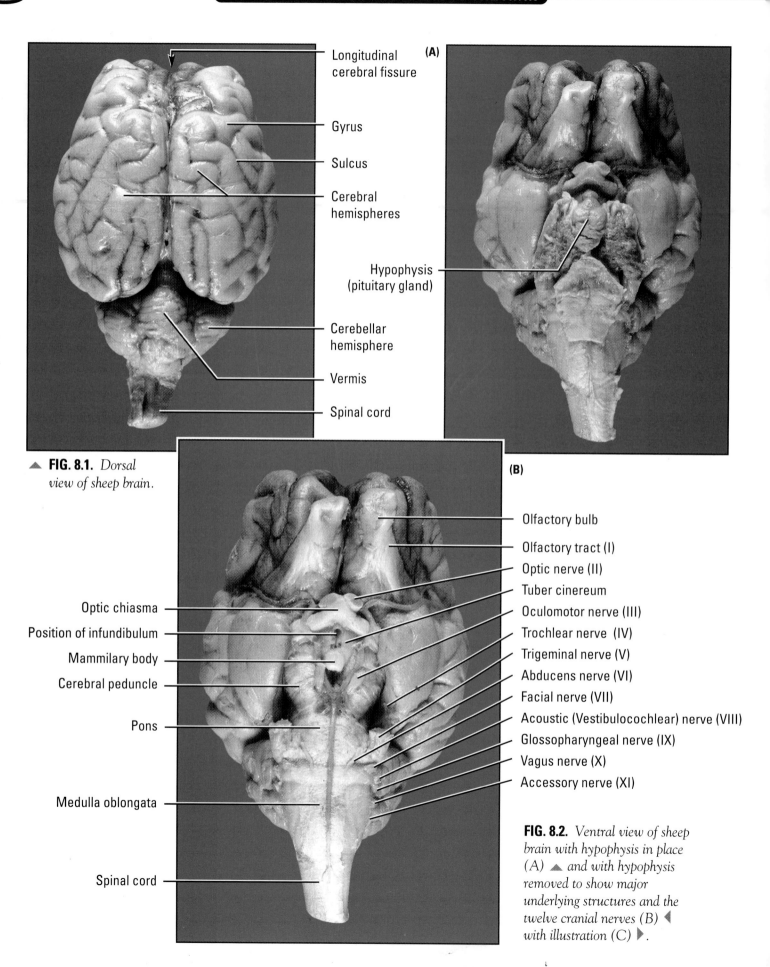

Longitudinal cerebral fissure

Gyrus

Sulcus

Cerebral hemispheres

Hypophysis (pituitary gland)

Cerebellar hemisphere

Vermis

Spinal cord

(A)

▲ **FIG. 8.1.** *Dorsal view of sheep brain.*

(B)

Olfactory bulb

Olfactory tract (I)

Optic nerve (II)

Tuber cinereum

Oculomotor nerve (III)

Trochlear nerve (IV)

Trigeminal nerve (V)

Abducens nerve (VI)

Facial nerve (VII)

Acoustic (Vestibulocochlear) nerve (VIII)

Glossopharyngeal nerve (IX)

Vagus nerve (X)

Accessory nerve (XI)

Optic chiasma

Position of infundibulum

Mammilary body

Cerebral peduncle

Pons

Medulla oblongata

Spinal cord

FIG. 8.2. *Ventral view of sheep brain with hypophysis in place (A) ▲ and with hypophysis removed to show major underlying structures and the twelve cranial nerves (B) ◄ with illustration (C) ▶.*

voluntary movements. The parts of the brain responsible for higher functions like memory and learning are located in the cerebrum. The cerebrum is composed of several regions (or lobes): the frontal lobe, the temporal lobe, the parietal lobe and the occipital lobe. The **frontal lobe** primarily controls fine movements and is responsible for "higher" functions such as language, memory, emotional expression and personality. The **temporal lobe** processes auditory signals and some visual information. The **parietal lobe** handles basic body information provided by touch receptors, muscle receptors and joint receptors. The **occipital lobe** processes visual information. Caudal to the cerebrum is the smaller cerebellum which also possesses gyri and sulci. The cerebellum consists of two lateral hemispheres which border a medial **vermis**. The **cerebellum** is primarily a reflex center for the integration of skeletal muscle movements. It is responsible for such activities as muscle coordination and balance. At the base of the cerebellum, locate the brainstem or **medulla oblongata**. This is the most caudal portion of the brain and leads directly into the **spinal cord**. The medulla oblongata regulates many autonomic functions such as breathing, heart rate, digestion, sweating and vomiting.

On the ventral aspect of the brain, several other structures are visible (Figure 8.2). Moving from the medulla oblongata cranially, identify the **pons** (the enlarged portion of the medulla oblongata ventral to the cerebellum), the **hypothalamus-pituitary complex** and the stalk of the **infundibulum** which supports the pituitary gland. The role of the hypothalamus-pituitary complex is discussed in detail in Chapter 9. Moving rostrally from the infundibulum, you will see the juncture where the **optic nerves** enter the brain, the **optic chiasma**. Notice they appear to fuse together and cross at the optic chiasma. This is a morphological "illusion" that does not correspond to the actual internal arrangement of the nerve fibers within the optic nerves. In fact, nerve fibers leading from the nasal (or inner) halves of each retina cross to the opposite hemisphere of the brain, while nerve fibers leading from the temporal (or outside) halves of each retina do not. Thus information from our right and left visual fields (but not right and left eyes!) remains separated throughout its journey into and through the brain. As a result, information from the right visual field is decoded by the left occipital lobe of the brain and information from the left visual field is decoded by the right occipital lobe. Although we don't

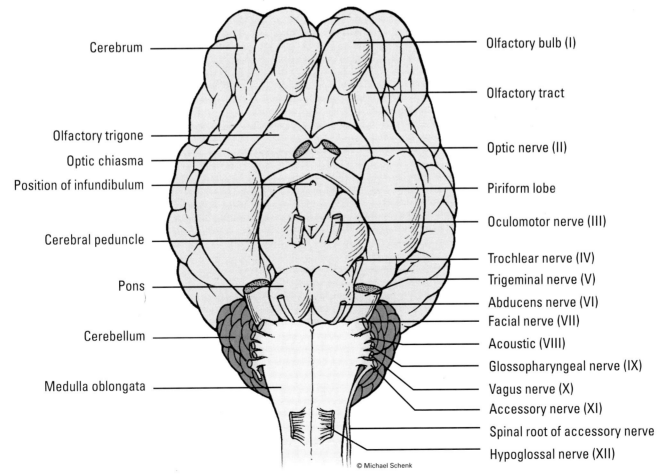

▲ **FIG. 8.2C.** *Ventral view of sheep brain with hypophysis removed (illustration).*

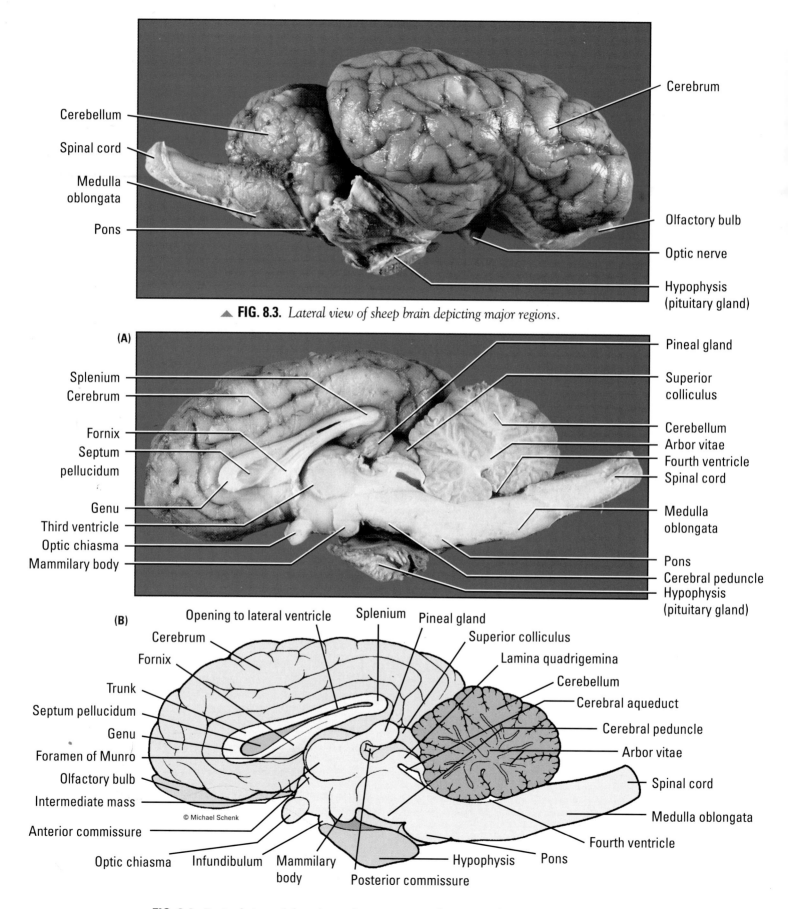

▲ **FIG. 8.3.** *Lateral view of sheep brain depicting major regions.*

▲ **FIG. 8.4.** *Sagittal view of sheep brain depicting internal anatomy (A) with illustration (B).*

often think of them as such, our eyes (at least the photoreceptors and intermediate ganglia of the retina) are actually extensions of our brain, much like the olfactory bulbs located in the nasal region. Very basic processing of visual information actually starts in the retina, long before the stimuli reach the optic lobes of the brain. Just dorsal to the optic nerves are the **olfactory tracts**. Depending on how far rostrally you proceeded when removing the brain (if you are using the mink brain), you may be fortunate enough to see the **olfactory bulbs** at the end of each olfactory tract. (If you are using a prepared sheep brain, the olfactory bulbs will lie on the ventral portion of the cerebrum at the anterior end of the brain.)

CRANIAL NERVES

Along the ventral aspect of the brain, all twelve cranial nerves can be found emanating from their respective regions of the brain and brainstem (Figure 8.2 and Table 8.1). Moving from the front of the brain caudally, the first set of cranial nerves are the **olfactory nerves** (I), large sensory nerve tracts emanating from the cribiform plate of the cranium and projecting rostrally into the sensory cells of the nasal epithelium. Next are the **optic nerves** (II) which bifurcate outside the brain and pass through the optic foramena where they innervate the retina as sensory fibers. Traces of the **oculomotor nerves** (III) may be found at the lateral margins of the infundibulum, where they leave the brain, pass through the foramen rotundum and innervate the dorsal, ventral and medial rectus and ventral oblique muscles of the eye as well as the ciliary bodies. The oculomotor nerves have both sensory and motor components. The **trochlear nerves** (IV) are extremely small fibers which project rostrally from the anterior-most portion of the medulla oblongata. Having both sensory and motor functions, these nerves innervate the dorsal oblique eye muscles. The trochlear nerves are unique in that they are the only cranial nerves that originate from the dorsal surface of the brain. The largest of the cranial nerves, the **trigeminal nerve** (V), consists of three branches (ophthalmic, maxillary and mandibular branches) which emanate from the posterior portion of the pons. The **ophthalmic branch** innervates facial skin near the eye and nose, the **maxillary branch** innervates the jaw muscles, and the **mandibular branch** innervates the lower lip, tongue, teeth, lower jaw and the major muscles of mastication. The trigeminal nerve thus has sensory and motor capabilities. The remaining cranial nerves (VI–XII) all originate from the medulla oblongata. The **abducens nerves** (VI) innervate the lateral rectus and retractor bulbi muscles of the eye and provide both sensory and motor inputs to that region. The **facial nerves** (VII) exit the skull through the stylomastoid foramen and innervate the facial and digastric muscles, the anterior two-thirds of the taste buds, and

the mandibular, sublingual and lacrimal glands. The **acoustic nerve** (VIII) (also called the vestibulocochlear or auditory nerve) has two branches: the **vestibular branch** which innervates the inner ear organs responsible for providing information on equilibrium and orientation, and the **cochlear branch** which innervates the organs responsible for sound detection. Thus the acoustic nerve provides sensory information only. The remaining cranial nerves (IX–XII) all provide both sensory and motor information. The **glossopharyngeal nerve** (IX) innervates the pharyngeal muscles and posterior one-third of the tongue. The **vagus nerve** (X) innervates the pharynx, larynx, heart, lungs, diaphragm and abdominal organs. The **accessory nerve** (XI) innervates the muscles of the neck and upper shoulders and the **hypoglossal nerve** (XII) innervates muscles of the throat and tongue.

BRACHIAL PLEXUS

The spinal cord is greatly enlarged in the upper thoracic region of quadrupeds (cranial to the 1st rib) to accommodate the confluence of nerves associated with the transmission of motor impulses to the forelimbs. This pattern is repeated in the lumbar region as well to accommodate the large number of motor nerves leading to the hindlimbs. The ventral roots of the 6th, 7th and 8th cervical nerves and the 1st thoracic nerve constitute a complex network known as the **brachial plexus** (Figure 8.5)

INSTRUCTION

To expose the brachial plexus, remove the superficial brachial muscles (sternomastoid, pectoralis major, pectoralis minor) and carefully clean away the fat and fascia from the nerves. It may be helpful to remove some of the blood vessels associated with this region to completely uncover the nerves. Begin at the cranial end of the plexus and work caudally. Identify and isolate each nerve in the plexus by separating it from its neighboring tissue starting in the more distal portion of the limb and working toward the median plane of the body. Concentrate on one side of the mink (e.g., right side), since the plexus is symmetrical across both sides of the body.

As a beginning point of reference, locate the **vagus nerve** which runs longitudinally along each side of the entire length of the trachea. The **first, second** and **third cervical nerves** may be difficult to locate due to their short lengths and close association with neighboring tissue. The **fourth cervical nerve** runs very closely to the third. The **fifth and sixth cervical nerves** contribute to the formation of the **phrenic nerve** running alongside the vagus nerve for much

TABLE 8.1. *Cranial nerves of the mink.*

NUMBER	NAME	SENSORY	MOTOR	SUPERFICIAL ORIGIN ON BRAIN	DISTRIBUTION
I	Olfactory	x		Pyriform lobe lateral to optic chiasma	Neurosensory cells of nasal epithelium
II	Optic	x		Cerebrum near cranial end of hypothalamus	Sensory fibers of retina
III	Oculomotor	x	x	Cerebral peduncles	Dorsal, ventral and medial rectus and ventral oblique muscles of the eye
IV	Trochlear	x	x	Dorsal surface of mesencephalon anterior to pons	Dorsal oblique eye muscle
V	Trigeminal	x	x	Posterior portion of pons	**Ophthalmic branch** innervates facial skin near eye and nose; **Maxillary branch** innervates jaw muscles; **Mandibular branch** innervates lower lip, tongue, teeth, lower jaw and muscles of mastication
VI	Abducens	x	x	Medulla oblongata	Lateral rectus and retractor bulbi eye muscles
VII	Facial	x	x	Medulla oblongata	Facial and digastric muscles, sensory innervation of taste buds (anterior two-thirds), mandibular, sublingual, and lacrimal glands
VIII	Acoustic	x		Medulla oblongata	Sensory hair cells of inner ear and semicircular canals
IX	Glossopharyngeal	x	x	Medulla oblongata	Pharyngeal muscles and tongue (posterior one-third)
X	Vagus	x	x	Medulla oblongata	Pharynx, larynx, heart, lungs, diaphragm and stomach
XI	Accessory	x	x	Medulla oblongata	Cleidomastoid, sternomastoid and trapezius muscles
XII	Hypoglossal	x	x	Medulla oblongata	Muscles of the throat and tongue

of its length. The sixth cervical nerve also gives rise to the **suprascapular nerve** associated with the supraspinatus and subscapularis muscles. The **first subscapular nerve**, the **axillary nerve** and the **musculocutaneous nerve** are divergences of the **sixth** and **seventh cervical nerves**. The sixth, seventh and **eighth cervical nerves** and the **first thoracic nerve** give rise to the **radial nerve** which innervates the extensors of the forelimb. The seventh and eighth cervical nerve and the first thoracic nerve give rise

to the **median nerve** which innervates many forearm flexors. The **ulnar** and **posterior ventral thoracic nerves** both arise from the eighth cervical and first thoracic nerve. The ulnar nerve innervates flexor muscles of the forelimb, while the posterior ventral thoracic nerve innervates the pectoral muscles.

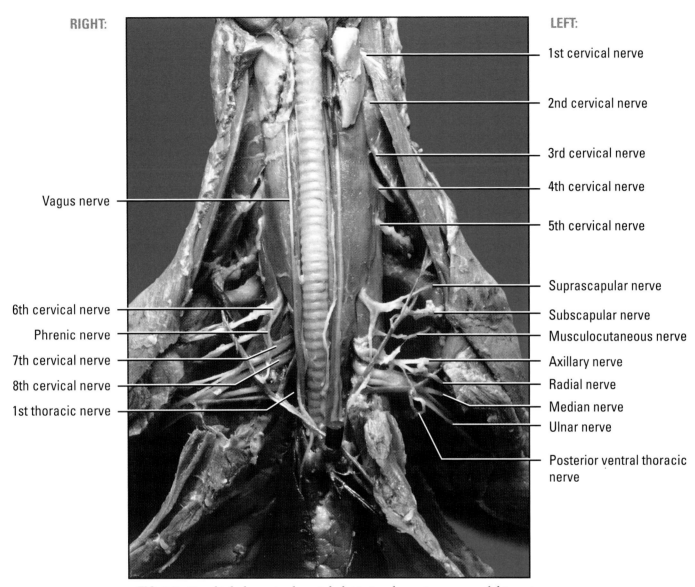

RIGHT:

LEFT:

1st cervical nerve

2nd cervical nerve

3rd cervical nerve

4th cervical nerve

5th cervical nerve

Suprascapular nerve

Subscapular nerve

Musculocutaneous nerve

Axillary nerve

Radial nerve

Median nerve

Ulnar nerve

Posterior ventral thoracic nerve

Vagus nerve

6th cervical nerve

Phrenic nerve

7th cervical nerve

8th cervical nerve

1st thoracic nerve

▲ **FIG. 8.5.** *Brachial plexus in the mink depicting the major nerves of this region.*

THE EYE

The eye is a complex sensory organ specialized to receive external stimuli (in the form of light waves) and convert this light energy into chemical information that can be integrated (to some extent by the eye, itself) and sent to the brain for interpretation. Since minks have eyes that are quite small, you should dissect the eye of a sheep (or cow) to acquire an appreciation for the intricate structures that play a role in the vision of mammals. Many of the anatomical features of the sheep eye are, in fact, quite similar to those of the human eye.

INSTRUCTION

*Begin by removing the fatty tissue that covers a large part of the eye. You will encounter bands of muscle tissue and glands that **should not be removed**.*

Be careful not to puncture through the surface of the eye while preparing the external surface. With forceps, locate the optic nerve (on the opposite side of the eye from the clear cornea) and trim the fatty tissue away from it, being careful not to damage the optic nerve or adjacent musculature.

External Anatomy

Mammalian eyes contain six major extrinsic ocular muscles, which collectively control the intricate movements of the eyes and permit a mammal to move its eyes and track moving objects or change its field of vision without (necessarily) moving its head (Figure 8.6). To identify these muscles correctly, it is imperative to determine whether your eye is a "right eye" or a "left eye." The **ventral oblique** muscle (found on the bottom of the eyeball) is the only muscle that naturally "hugs" the circumference of the eye and is the key to determining which eye you have (see Table 8.2). Its insertion is on the side of the eyeball near the insertion of the **lateral rectus** muscle. So, by viewing the eyeball from the front, if the ventral oblique muscle wraps around toward *your* left to meet the lateral rectus, you are holding a right eye. If the ventral oblique muscle wraps toward *your* right to the meet the lateral rectus, you have a left eye.

In determining the orientation of your eyeball, you have already identified two of the six muscles. On the left eye the **ventral oblique** muscle is responsible for rotating the eye counterclockwise (clockwise on the right eye) and the **lateral rectus** muscle rotates the eye laterally. Next, identify the **ventral rectus** which rotates the eye ventrally, the **dorsal rectus** which rotates the eye dorsally and the **medial rectus** which rotates the eye medially. On the left eye the **dorsal oblique** muscle rotates the eye clockwise (counterclockwise on the right eye). These are the six major muscles that contribute to the rotational movements of the eye. Adjacent to the dorsal rectus is the **levator palpebrae superior** muscle which elevates the entire eyeball. You may find a large gland attached to the levator palpebrae superior. This is the **lacrimal gland** which secretes the lubricating liquid we know as tears. This secretion keeps the eyeball moist and dust-free. In some mammals (not humans) there is another muscle, known as the **retractor bulbi**, that surrounds the projecting optic nerve and is responsible for retracting the eyeball into the eye socket. Many mammals have other accessory glands associated with the eye that are absent in humans. **Tarsal glands** (found underneath the eyelids), **infraorbital glands** (small salivary glands which drain into the mouth), and **harderian glands** (which also bathe the eyeball much like the lacrimal glands) are present in other mammals.

▶ **FIG. 8.6.**
Extrinsic ocular muscles.

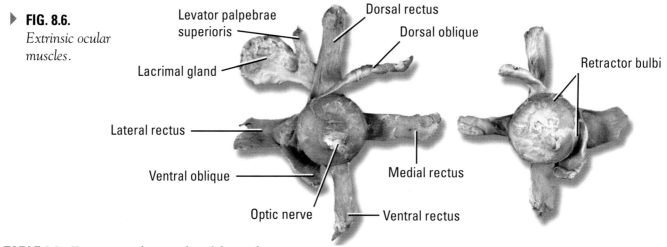

TABLE 8.2. *Extrinsic ocular muscles of the mink.*

NAME	INNERVATION BY	ATTACHMENT	ACTION
Dorsal rectus	Oculomotor (III)	Dorsal midline	Rotates eye dorsally
Dorsal oblique	Trochlear (IV)	Anterior, dorsomedial border of eyeball	Rotates left eye clockwise
Lateral rectus	Abducens (VI)	Lateral border of eyeball	Rotates eye laterally
Levator palpebrae superior	Oculomotor (III)	Connective tissue dorsal to eyeball	Elevates eyeball
Medial rectus	Oculomotor (III)	Medial border of eyeball	Rotates eye medially
Ventral rectus	Oculomotor (III)	Ventral midline	Rotates eye ventrally
Ventral oblique	Oculomotor (III)	Anterior, ventrolateral border of eyeball	Rotates left eye counter clockwise

Many mammals, including minks, also possess a "third eyelid" that may still be present on your preserved eye. This eyelid, which is clear and remains invisible when closed, is known as the **nictitating membrane**. Humans lack a nictitating membrane; however a vestigial remnant of this structure is present. Identify the **cornea**—a tough, transparent layer that allows light to enter the eye while protecting the underlying structures (Figure 8.7). The cornea is composed of a special lamellar arrangement of cells that permits nearly perfect optical transparency. This property comes with a price however. The cells of the cornea must continuously pump out their interstitial fluid to maintain the proper structural arrangement necessary for clear vision. The **optic nerve** in the back of the eye is the site at which the axons of all the photoreceptors contained in the retina converge and send their information from the eye to the brain (Figure 8.6). The optic nerve is continuous with the retina on the inner surface of the eye. Surrounding the remainder of the eye (exclusive of the cornea) and the optic nerve is a tough, white layer of tissue called the **sclera** (Figure 8.7). The sclera also helps protect the eye from damage.

Internal Anatomy

INSTRUCTION

Using scissors, carefully cut the eye in half through its frontal plane (giving you one half containing the cornea and iris and one half with the sclera and the optic nerve). Place the eye in your dissecting tray with the cornea facing up and gently open it by lifting the front half.

Inside the eye you should see the lens floating in a fluid-filled chamber known as the **vitreous chamber**. The fluid contained in this chamber is a mixture of water, called the **vitreous humor**, and fine transparent fibers suspended in the fluid. The **lens** is a fairly solid, biconvex structure composed of concentric sheets of clear cells (arranged much like the skin of an onion) (Figure 8.8 and 8.9). While

quite sturdy, the lens is flexible and capable of b[...] focus the image on the **retina** at the back of the eyeball. Small intrinsic muscles known as **ciliary bodies** attached to the lens accomplish this task. The retina diminishes in thickness from back to front, terminating at the margin of the ciliary bodies, identified by the scalloped junction known as the **ora serrata**. This region marks the division between the anterior portion of the retina and the ciliary bodies. The rods and cones (photoreceptors) are imbedded in the retina. The back of the retina is covered with a reflective membrane called the **choroid layer** which enhances the amount of light that is reflected back into the rods and cones of the eye (Figure 8.10). One of the most amazing features of the mammalian eye is the way in which the photoreceptors are arranged. The rods and cones are actually on the inside of the retina (the side toward the lens) but face away from the lens. Thus light must pass through them and bounce off the choroid layer of the retina back toward the lens before it is detected by the rods and cones! It is imperative that the rods, cones and other associated nerve cells in the retina be absolutely optically clear so that distortion of the visible light rays entering the eye and passing through them is minimal.

The distribution of photoreceptor types in the mink is quite different from that in humans. The retina of most primates contains around 120–130 million cones and 6–8 million rods. Minks, being primarily nocturnal creatures, have an abundance of **rods** in their retinas, giving their eyes enhanced sensitivity to dim light. The price they pay for this increased ability to see well at night is a reduction in the ability to detect colors and, to some degree, a reduction in visual acuity—both consequences associated with the absence of **cones** (the color-sensing photoreceptors). Because many rods converge on a single intermediate ganglion in the retina, there is a convergence, or pooling, of receptor information from rods. This pooling of information increases the likelihood of the common intermediate ganglion reaching the level of excitation necessary to send an impulse to the brain. In addition, a single rod requires less light energy for activation than a single cone. These two features of rods

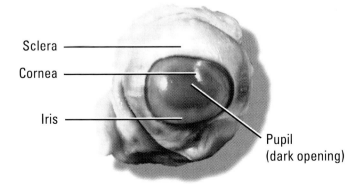

Sclera
Cornea
Iris
Pupil
(dark opening)

▲ **FIG. 8.7.** *External anatomy of the eye.*

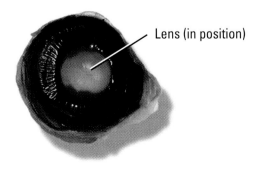

Lens (in position)

▲ **FIG. 8.8.** *Lens (in place).*

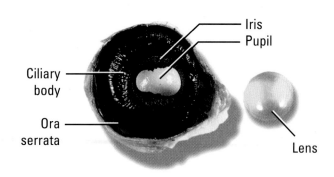

Iris
Pupil
Ciliary body
Ora serrata
Lens

▲ **FIG. 8.9.** *Layers of the eye.*

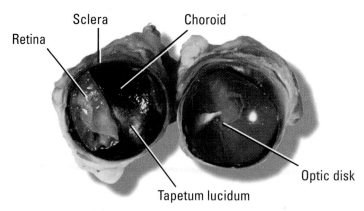

Sclera
Choroid
Retina
Optic disk
Tapetum lucidum

▲ **FIG. 8.10.** *Internal anatomy of the eye.*

aid in sensitivity to low levels of light, but due to the pooling of visual information, detract from image resolution. Generally animals possessing primarily rods in their retinas are extremely adept at detecting movement in their visual field, even when that movement generates only a faint image on the retina. This aspect contributes to a predator's ability to "spot" its prey at a great distance and the obvious need for it to stalk its prey in a slow, stealthy manner, for many prey also possess similar visual abilities.

In animals with color vision (like humans), the distribution of cones is restricted to the **fovea** (or focal point), a small region of densely packed cones in the retina. Because there are very few cones in the periphery of the human eye, we are actually completely color-blind in our peripheral visual field. The fact that we "experience" a world with colors 360° around us is because our brains "fill in" the regions of our peripheral vision that lack the ability to detect color with recently gathered images from the foveal regions of our ever-moving eyes. Since color perception is a subjective experience, it is quite easy for the cerebral cortex to make sense of our visual world by imparting a sense of color consistency to our surroundings. (Try this experiment: Have someone mix several colored pencils or beads together in their hand while standing behind you. It's even better if you don't know the colors they have. Pick a small focal point on a wall several feet in front of you and DO NOT MOVE YOUR EYES. Then instruct them to choose one color randomly and *slowly* move the object around your head into your peripheral vision and continue *slowly* moving it in front of you until you correctly identify the color. You should notice that you will detect the presence of the object long before you will be able to distinguish its color!) Because of the dense conglomeration of cones in the fovea, it is devoid of any blood vessels and intermediate ganglia and therefore has the most unimpeded vision of any place in the eye. This tight packing of receptors at the fovea contributes to the high visual acuity we perceive when we look directly at an object. The colloquial phrase "eyes like a hawk" has its roots

in the anatomy of the hawk's retina. Hawks, eagles and other birds of prey actually possess two foveae in each eye—one in the center of the eye (pointing forward) and one in the periphery of the eye (pointing to the side). Thus hawks and eagles are able to perceive extreme details in their peripheral vision.

Many mammals have a special coating on the choroid layer of the retina known as the **tapetum lucidum** which gives these mammals their traditional "eyeshine" when spotted at night by flashlight or in the headlights of a car (Figure 8.10). This special layer increases the light gathering ability of the eye and endows these mammals with enhanced night vision. The mink possesses a tapetum lucidum, and thus has a characteristic yellowish-green eyeshine. Humans lack a tapetum lucidum and therefore do not demonstrate eyeshine at night. At one spot on the retina you should be able to distinguish the position where the optic nerve exits the back of the eye. This spot is called the **optic disk**. There are no photoreceptors on the surface of the retina at this point, and this confluence of nerves is responsible for the visual phenomenon known as the "blind spot." The opening in front of the lens is known as the **pupil**. A thin sheet of tissue suspended between the cornea and the lens surrounds this opening. This is the **iris** which contains two groups of smooth muscles (circular and radiating) which contract to change the size of the pupil opening and consequently regulate the amount of light which enters the eye. When the circular fibers contract, the pupil becomes smaller; when the radiating fibers contract, the pupil enlarges. The chamber between the iris and cornea is called the **anterior chamber** and is filled with a liquid called the **aqueous humor**. The aqueous fluid is secreted by the ciliary bodies and continuously drains into a sinus surrounding the eye, but the net volume of this fluid remains at a constant level. Its presence enhances the optical properties of the lens by providing resistance to keep the lens in place while delivering valuable oxygen and nutrients to the region and removing metabolic by-products of nearby tissues.

Endocrine System

LABORATORY OBJECTIVES

After completing this chapter,
you should be able to:

1. Identify the major endocrine
glands of the mink and their
respective locations in the
body.
2. Identify the hormones
produced by each endocrine
gland and their functions.
3. Recognize the microanatomy
of the endocrine glands.

The complex actions and interactions of organ systems in vertebrates must be precisely controlled to meet the specific needs of the animal. You have already examined one of the major systems responsible for coordinating these processes—the nervous system. The endocrine system is another major player in the body's attempt to coordinate the activities of its many organs and organ systems. In that respect, the endocrine and nervous systems are very much alike. The similarities between the two systems do not go very far beyond that, however. Unlike the nervous system which has its own contained system for information transfer (the nerves), the endocrine system is ductless and therefore must rely on another neighboring system to send its messages throughout the body. The glands of the endocrine system produce and secrete their hormones directly into the bloodstream to be carried to their target organs. These **hormones** are chemical compounds that interact with target cells in the body to produce a myriad of behavioral, neurological and physiological responses. In this way, they influence many of the same behaviors and processes that the nervous system regulates. However, due to the nature of hormones, the effects produced by the endocrine system are generally not short-lived. Nervous responses are instantaneous and degrade immediately, but hormones circulating through the bloodstream may take some time to produce a response and anywhere from minutes to hours to break down. Thus hormonal effects tend to be much longer in duration and the processes that are under hormonal control are typically processes that occur over hours, days, weeks or even years (e.g., sexual maturation, metabolic rate, growth rate, ovulation). In addition, the degree of response shown by the target organ is directly proportional to the amount of hormone released by the endocrine gland—the more hormone a gland releases, the more pronounced the effect. This is a fundamental distinction from the all-or-nothing response of nerve cells and illustrates why both systems, the nervous system and the endocrine system, are essential for complex organisms to coordinate different aspects of their lives (Figure 9.1).

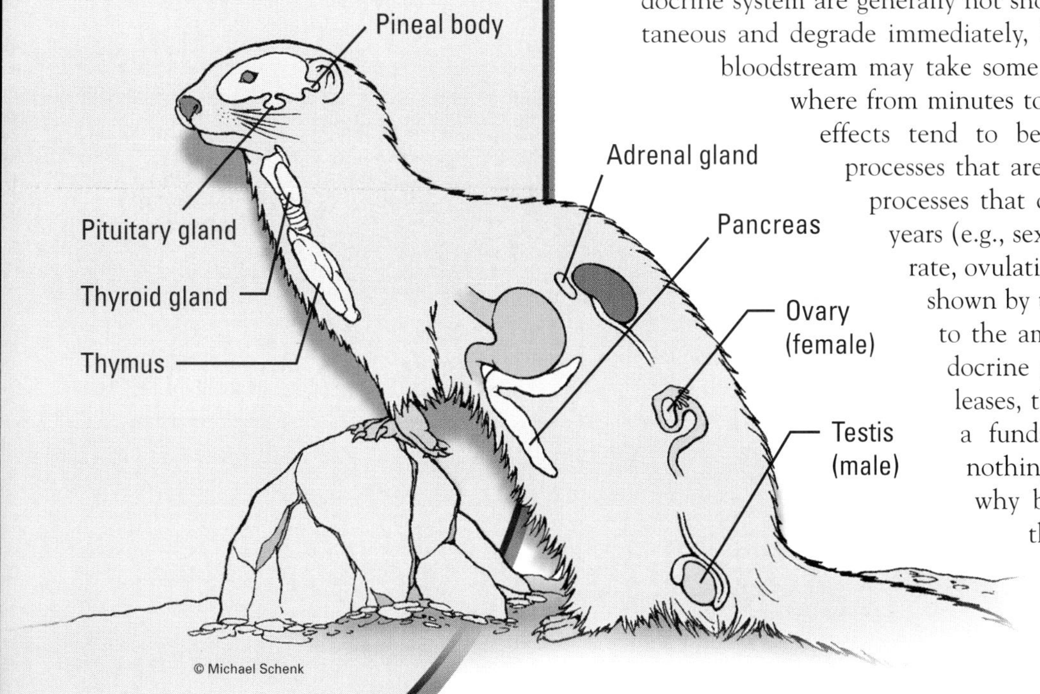

FIG. 9.1. *Illustration of endocrine glands in the mink depicting their approximate locations.*

CRANIAL AND THORACIC REGIONS

You have already identified some of the organs discussed in this chapter. That is because organs that function in the endocrine system often have other tissue in them that functions in the digestive system (pancreas), nervous system (hypothalamus-pituitary complex) or reproductive system (ovaries and testes). The centralized control center of the endocrine system is the **hypothalamus-pituitary complex** of the brain (Figure 9.2). (You will only be able to see this organ if you extensively dissect the mink brain or opt to use commercially-prepared sheep brains.) Associated with the pituitary gland is the **pineal body**, a small bulb located on the midbrain which produces **melatonin**, a hormone which regulates body functions related to the seasonal day length. The hypothalamus-pituitary complex produces many hormones which, in turn, stimulate the activity of many of the other endocrine glands in the body. Likewise, other endocrine organs may produce hormones that stimulate or inhibit regions of the pituitary gland or hypothalamus. By this feedback mechanism, the endocrine system is able to turn itself on and off in response to environmental or endogenous stimuli.

Pituitary Gland

The pituitary gland is actually composed of two distinct regions in mammals—the **anterior pituitary** (adenohypophysis) and the **posterior pituitary** (neurohypophysis) (Figure 9.2). The anterior pituitary is composed of endocrine cells that synthesize and secrete a number of hormones into the bloodstream. However, it is the hypothalamus which regulates the release of these hormones through

secretions of releasing hormones or inhibiting hormones into the capillary network adjacent to the pituitary gland. Among the major hormones produced by the anterior pituitary gland are: **growth hormone, prolactin, follicle-stimulating hormone, luteinizing hormone, thyroid-stimulating hormone**, and **adrenocorticotropic hormone**. The posterior pituitary, unlike its neighbor, is really an extension of the brain composed primarily of neurosecretory cells that store and secrete two peptide hormones: oxytocin and antidiuretic hormone. **Oxytocin** stimulates contractions of the uterus and mammary gland cells, while **antidiuretic hormone** promotes water retention in the kidney. For a complete description of the functions of the pituitary hormones, see Table 9.1.

Thymus and Thyroid Glands

Examine the ventral aspect of the neck region of your mink. Along either side of the trachea just caudal to the larynx, identify the two sections of the **thyroid gland** (Figure 9.3A). The thyroid gland produces two hormones: **thyroxine** which controls the growth rate and metabolic rate of the organism and **calcitonin** which lowers the organism's blood calcium levels. Follow the trachea caudally and locate the **thymus gland**, near the cranial margin of the heart but outside the pericardial membrane (Figure 9.3B). The color and texture of this gland should differ sufficiently from neighboring lung tissue to permit easy identification. The thymus gland produces **thymosin**, a hormone that stimulates the development of the immune system.

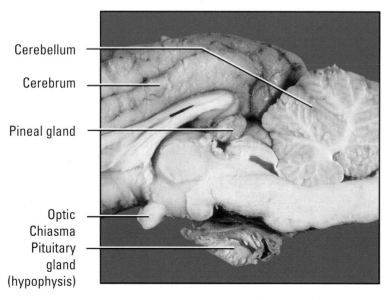

FIG. 9.2. *Pituitary gland and pineal body.*

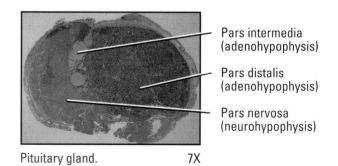
Pituitary gland.   7X

(A)

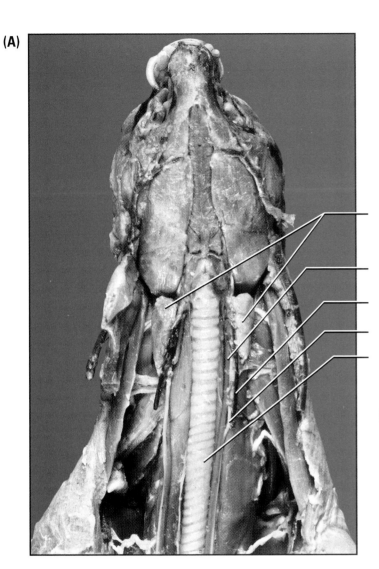

◀ **FIG. 9.3.** *Thyroid glands (A) and thymus (B).*

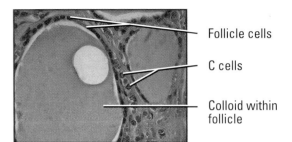

Follicle cells

C cells

Colloid within follicle

Thyroid gland.   400X

Thyroid gland

Common carotid artery

Internal jugular vein

Vagus nerve

Trachea

(B)

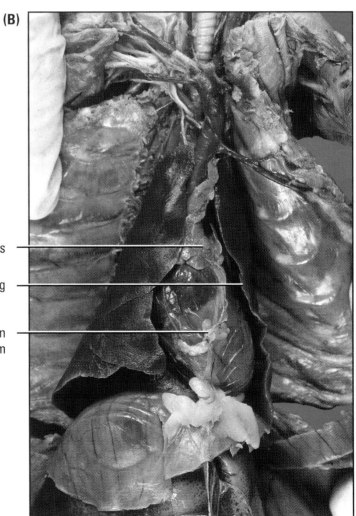

Thymus

Lung

Heart in pericardium

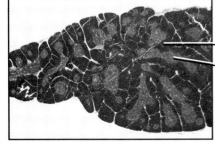

Cortex

Medulla

Thymus.   7X

TABLE 9.1. *Endocrine glands, hormone products and their functions in mammals.*

ENDOCRINE GLAND	HORMONE PRODUCED	HORMONE FUNCTION
Hypothalamus		Regulates other endocrine glands
Anterior pituitary (adenohypophysis)	Growth hormone	Stimulates growth and metabolic functions
	Prolactin	Stimulates milk production and secretion
	Follicle-stimulating hormone	Stimulates sperm and ova production
	Luteinizing hormone	Stimulates testes and ovaries
	Thyroid-stimulating hormone	Stimulates thyroid gland
	Adrenocorticotropic hormone	Stimulates adrenal cortex to secrete steroid hormones and endorphins
Posterior pituitary (neurohypophysis)	Oxytocin	Stimulates contractions of uterus and mammary gland cells
	Antidiuretic hormone	Promotes water retention in kidneys
Pineal body	Melatonin	Controls body functions related to photoperiod and seasonal day length and influences sexual maturation
Thymus	Thymosin	Stimulates immune system
Thyroid	Thyroxine	Controls metabolism and growth rates
	Calcitonin	Lowers blood calcium levels
Pancreas	Insulin	Lowers blood glucose levels
	Glucagon	Raises blood glucose levels
	Somatostatin	Inhibits release of insulin and glucagon
Adrenal	Epinephrine and norepinephrine	Mediate responses to stressful situations
	Corticosteroids	Control carbohydrate and protein metabolism
	Aldosterone	Controls blood pressure
Testes (male)	Testosterone	Maintains male sexual characteristics, sperm production and sex drive
Ovaries (female)	Estrogen	Induces maturation of oocytes and ovulation; initiates thickening of uterine lining
	Progesterone	Increases thickening of uterine lining; causes negative feedback which promotes disintegration of corpus luteum

ABDOMINAL REGION

Pancreas

Locate the **pancreas** (identified earlier as a digestive gland) (Figure 9.4). The pancreas also functions in the endocrine system by producing **insulin** and **glucagon** which lower and raise blood glucose levels, respectively, and **somatostatin** which regulates the levels of insulin and glucagon in the blood. Insulin acts primarily on the liver, stimulating it to store more glucose in the form of glycogen, and to a lesser degree on the individual cells of the body, promoting a higher degree of glucose usage. Glucagon works as an antagonist to insulin and reverses the body's actions in these areas. Somatostatin inhibits the release of both insulin and glucagon by the pancreas. There are specific regions of the pancreas known as **islets of Langerhans** which release hormones into the bloodstream through tiny openings that merge with blood vessels running through the pancreas.

Adrenal Glands

On the medial margin of each kidney (near the midline of the body), a small, oval-shaped gland is located. These are the **adrenal glands** which control such processes as blood pressure, carbohydrate metabolism and protein metabolism, and mediate responses to stressful situations (Figure 9.5). Like the kidney, the adrenal gland has a cortex and medulla region. Hormones from the cortical region control metabolic functions, while the medullar hormones prolong the actions of the sympathetic nervous system during stressful situations.

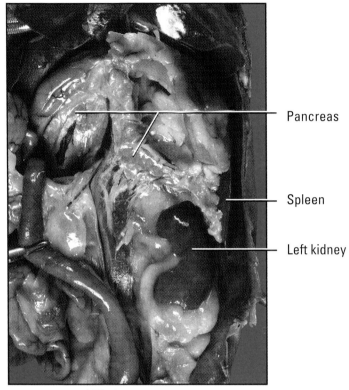

▲ **FIG. 9.4.** *Pancreas.*

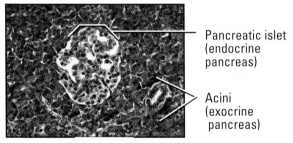

Pancreas (islet of Langerhans). 75X

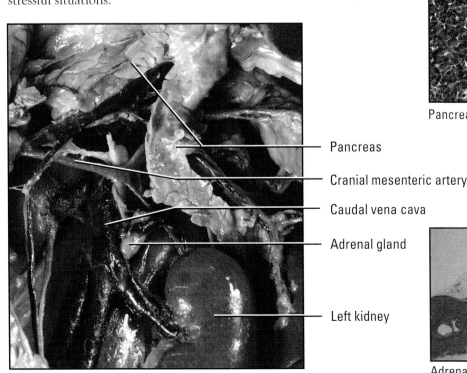

▲ **FIG. 9.5.** *Adrenal gland.*

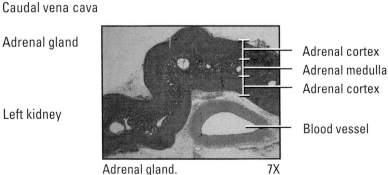

Adrenal gland.   7X

Testes and Ovaries

In females, the **ovaries** contain different types of hormone-producing tissues (Figure 9.6). When the oocyte has matured and ovulation is about to take place, **estrogen** levels rise triggering ovulation and the thickening of the uterine lining. Shortly after ovulation, the remnant tissue from which the oocyte erupted turns into the **corpus luteum** and begins to produce elevated levels of **progesterone**, the hormone that is responsible for increasing the thickness of the endometrial lining. As the levels of these two hormones decrease, the corpus luteum disintegrates and the onset of menstruation is triggered.

Within the **testes** of the male mink (Figure 9.7), special cells, known as **interstitial cells**, produce the hormone testosterone. Thus the testes are considered part of the endocrine system as well as the reproductive system. **Testosterone** is responsible for the development and maintenance of the male sexual characteristics and sex drive and the regulation of sperm production.

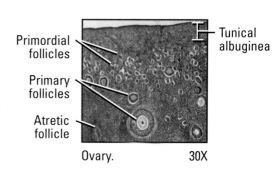

Primordial follicles

Primary follicles

Atretic follicle

Tunical albuginea

Ovary.   30X

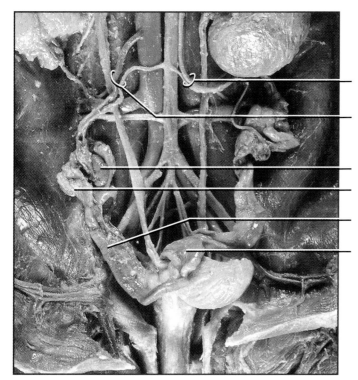

Left ovarian artery and vein

Right ovarian artery and vein

Ovary

Oviduct

Horn of uterus

Body of uterus

FIG. 9.6. *Ovaries.*

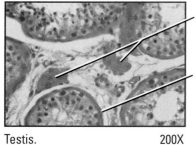

Interstitial (Leydig) cells

Seminiferous tubule

Testis.   200X

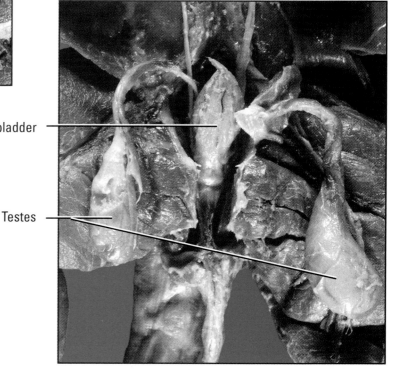

Urinary bladder

Testes

FIG. 9.7. *Testes.*

References

Burt, W. H. and R. P. Grossenheider. 1980. *A Field Guide to the Mammals: North America North of Mexico* (3rd ed.). Houghton Mifflin: Boston, MA.

Campbell, N. A. 1996. *Biology* (4th ed.). Benjamin/Cummings: Menlo Park, CA.

Crouch, J. E. 1969. *Text-Atlas of Cat Anatomy*. Lea and Febiger: Philadelphia, PA.

Dyce, K. M., W. O. Sack, and C. J. G. Wensing. 1987. *Textbook of Veterinary Anatomy*. W. B. Saunders: Philadelphia, PA.

Evans, H. E. and G. Christensen. 1979. *Miller's Anatomy of the Dog*. W. B. Saunders: Philadelphia, PA.

Kalat, J. W. 1988. *Biological Psychology* (3rd ed.). Wadsworth: Belmont, CA.

Radke, W. J. and R. B. Chiasson. 1998. *Laboratory Anatomy of the Mink*. McGraw-Hill: Boston, MA.

Sabastiani, A. M. and D. W. Fishbeck. 1998. *Mammalian Anatomy: The Cat*. Morton Publishing: Englewood, CO.

Schiffman, H. R. 1990. *Sensation and Perception: An Integrated Approach* (3rd ed.). John, Wiley and Sons: New York, NY.

Van De Graaff, K. M. and J. L. Crawley. 1996. *A Photographic Atlas for the Anatomy and Physiology Laboratory* (3rd ed.). Morton Publishing: Englewood, CO.

Walker, W. F. Jr. 1987. *Functional Anatomy of the Vertebrates: An Evolutionary Perspective*. Saunders College Publishing: Philadelphia, PA.

Glossary

abdomen – region of the body between the thorax and pelvis that contains the viscera.

abducens nerve – (Cranial Nerve VI) sensory/motor nerve originating from the medulla oblongata and innervating the lateral rectus and retractor bulbi muscles of the eye.

abduct – to move away from the median plane of the body.

accessory nerve – (Cranial Nerve XI) sensory/motor nerve that innervates the muscles of the neck and upper shoulders.

acoustic nerve – (Cranial Nerve VIII) sensory nerve with two branches that innervate the inner ear organs.

adduct – to move toward the median plane of the body.

adrenal gland – endocrine gland located on medial side of the kidney that produces hormones which mediate responses to stressful situations and control blood pressure and carbohydrate and protein metabolism.

adrenocorticotropic hormone – pituitary hormone that stimulates the adrenal cortex to secrete steroid hormones and endorphins.

aldosterone – hormone produced by the adrenal gland that controls blood pressure by acting on the reabsorption of sodium ions by the kidney and regulating water flow into the kidney.

allantoic duct – tube passing through the umbilical cord of the fetus connecting it with the allantois in the uterus of the mother.

allantois – extra-embryonic sac that acts as a repository for metabolic wastes produced by the fetus during development.

alveoli – (singular = alveolus); multilobed air sacs that form the terminal ducts of the bronchioles of the lungs and serve as the surfaces for the exchange of carbon dioxide and oxygen.

amphiarthrosis – a joint that permits slight movement (e.g., gliding joints of the wrist).

amylase – enzyme component of saliva that breaks down starches.

anal sacs – scent glands located near the anus that produce a foul-smelling, musky secretion.

anterior chamber – fluid-filled region of the eye located between the cornea and the iris.

antidiuretic hormone – posterior pituitary hormone which promotes water retention in the kidneys.

anus – opening of the rectum through which undigested food particles (feces) are egested from the body.

aorta – large artery arising from the left ventricle that distributes blood to the regions of the body.

appendicular skeleton – portion of the skeletal system consisting of the pectoral and pelvic girdles and the forelimbs and hindlimbs.

aqueous humor – liquid component of the anterior chamber of the vertebrate eye.

artery – blood vessel that carries blood away from the heart.

articulation – juncture between two or more bones (usually a movable joint).

atlas – (1) the 1st cervical vertebra; modified for attachment with the skull. (2) a collection of illustrations, tables and text providing information on a topic.

atrium – (plural = atria); chamber of the heart that receives blood.

auricle – flap-like, outer region covering the cranial portion of the atrium.

axial skeleton - portion of the skeleton consisting of the skull, vertebral column and rib cage.

axis – (1) the 2nd cervical vertebra. (2) a straight line that bisects the body into two equal halves; usually along the longer portion of the body.

bacculum – (syn: os penis) bone found in the penis of many mammals which facilitates maintaining erection.

bicuspid valve – (also called mitral valve); valve of the mammalian heart that directs blood flow from the left atrium to the left ventricle; so named because it has two cusps.

bile – digestive fluid secreted by the liver and stored in the gallbladder; functions in the emulsification of fats in the duodenum.

bone – rigid connective tissue used to support the body; characterized by densely packed, hard, fibrous matrix composed of calcium salts surrounding osteocytes (bone producing cells).

Bowman's capsule – cup-shaped layer of epithelial tissue surrounding the glomerulus of the vertebrate nephron which receives the filtrate of the blood.

brachial plexus – complex network in the thoracic cavity formed by the confluence of the ventral roots of the 6th, 7th and 8th cervical nerves and the 1st thoracic nerve.

brachiocephalic trunk – major branch of the aorta that supplies blood to the head and upper trunk region of the body.

brain – part of the central nervous system responsible for processing and integrating nerve impulses gathered from all sensory organs and receptors and for initiating motor impulses.

bronchi – (singular = bronchus); major divisions of the trachea that supply oxygen (and remove carbon dioxide) from the lobes of the lungs.

bronchiole – finer subdivision of the bronchi that forms a branching arrangement and carries gases to and from the regions within the lobe of a lung.

bulbourethral glands – accessory glands of the male reproductive system located at the base of the penis and urethra that contribute fluid to the semen which aids in neutralizing the acidity of the vagina.

calcitonin – thyroid hormone responsible for lowering blood calcium levels.

capitulum – a knob-like swelling at the end of a bone.

cardiac muscle – type of muscle tissue that forms the walls of the heart; characterized by striated muscle fibers joined together with gap junctions called intercalated disks which relay each heartbeat.

cardiovascular – of or pertaining to the heart and vascular system.

cartilage – flexible connective tissue that is characterized by fibrous tissue surrounding individual chondrocytes (cartilage-producing cells).

caudal – situated more toward the posterior (tail) region of the body.

caudal vena cava – the major vein returning deoxygenated blood from the lower extremities of the body to the right atrium of the mammalian heart.

cecum – blind projection located at the junction of the ileum and colon that serves as a sac where fermentation of cellulose occurs. The cecum plays a prominent role in the digestive process of most herbivores, but is reduced in omnivores and carnivores.

central nervous system – portion of the nervous system consisting of the brain and spinal cord.

cerebellum – region of the vertebrate hindbrain that integrates the movements of skeletal muscles and controls coordination and balance.

cerebrum – the portion of the brain devoted to the integration of sensory impulses, learning, memory and voluntary movements; divided into two hemispheres and located in the upper portion of the cranial cavity.

cervix – constricted portion of the female reproductive tract between the opening to the uterus and the vagina.

chordae tendineae – tendinous fibers connecting the valves of the mammalian heart to the papillary muscles associated with the ventricles of the heart.

choroid layer – vascular coating of the eye located between the sclera and the retina.

chyme – fluid produced by the action of digestive enzymes from the stomach mixing with and dissolving ingested food particles.

ciliary body – small muscles associated with the lens in the vertebrate eye; responsible for changing the shape of the lens to focus on objects at different distances.

collecting duct – tubule of the mammalian kidney that receives filtrate from the convoluted tubules and loop of Henle and sends it to the ureter for transport out of the kidney; allows water to be reabsorbed by bloodstream producing a highly concentrated urine.

colon – portion of the large intestine extending from the cecum to the rectum that functions primarily in reabsorbing water that has been added during the digestive process.

common bile duct – tubule through which bile is transported from the liver to the gallbladder and from the gallbladder to the duodenum.

cone – photoreceptor located in the mammalian eye that detects color.

convoluted tubules – region of the mammalian nephron that permits reabsorption of water and salts by the bloodstream.

cornea – transparent outer layer of the eye.

coronary artery – one of several small arteries located on the ventral surface of the heart that supply freshly-oxygenated blood to the tissue of the heart.

corpus cavernosum – column of highly vascularized erectile tissue that contains large sinuses to accommodate the increase in blood flow to the penis during erection; there are two adjacent corpus cavernosa in the dorsal section of the penis.

corpus callosum – internal sheet of nerve fibers uniting the two cerebral hemispheres; located below the sagittal fissure.

corpus luteum – region of the mammalian ovary that forms after the mature oocyte has erupted from the ovary; produces progesterone.

corpus spongiosum – column of highly vascularized erectile tissue that comprises one of three regions of the penis; contains the urethra.

cortex – outer region of an organ; ìrenal cortexî refers to outermost layer of the kidney.

corticosteroids – hormones produced by the adrenal glands which control protein metabolism and carbohydrate metabolism.

cranial – situated toward the head region.

cranial vena cava – the major vein returning deoxygenated blood from the upper extremities of the body to the right atrium of the mammalian heart.

cremaster muscles – small muscles attached to the testes that retract the testes toward the abdominal cavity; function to keep testes at a constant temperature by controlling their proximity to the body wall.

cremasteric pouches – thin, membranous sacs that house the testes of mammals; usually enclosed within the scrotum.

cystic duct – tubule connecting the pancreas to the duodenum; digestive enzymes produced by the pancreas are secreted into the duodenum through this canal.

diaphragm – muscular sheet separating the thoracic and abdominal cavities; used to ventilate the lungs of mammals.

diarthrosis – a joint that permits very free movement between bones (e.g., spheroidal or condylar joints of the shoulder or leg).

digestion – process by which ingested food particles are broken down into smaller units that can be utilized by individual cells in the body.

digitigrade – type of locomotion characterized by walking on the tips of the toes (digits); body weight is supported primarily by the phalanges.

dissection – the process or act of uncovering and exposing tissues and organs of an animal by teasing apart or cutting structures.

distal – situated toward the outer extremity of the body, away from the median plane (e.g., your hand is distal to your shoulder).

dorsal – situated toward the back of the body, closer to the vertebral column.

dorsal aorta – descending portion of the aorta that runs caudally along the ventral surface of the vertebral column and carries oxygenated blood from the left ventricle to the caudal regions of the body.

ductus arteriosus – short connection joining the pulmonary trunk with the aorta which allows a portion of the blood from the pulmonary trunk to enter the aorta instead of flowing to the lungs; found only in the fetus.

duodenum – first portion of the small intestine; functions primarily in final stages of chemical digestion and begins the process of nutrient absorption.

ears – external sensory receptors that pick up airborne vibrations and send them to the brain where they are interpreted as sounds.

egestion – the process of expelling undigested food particles through the anus.

endocrine - pertaining to the endocrine systemósystem responsible for the production of hormones that communicate chemically with target organs through the bloodstream.

endoskeleton – a hard skeleton used for support that is embedded within the soft tissues of the body.

endothermy – condition in which an animal uses its own metabolic processes to maintain a constant internal body temperature.

epicondyle – a projection above or upon a condyle.

epididymis – highly coiled tubule system that cups around the testis and serves as a storage unit and transportation canal for mature sperm.

epiglottis – cartilaginous flap that covers the glottis to prevent food from entering the larynx and trachea when swallowing.

epinephrine – (also called adrenaline); hormone produced by the adrenal glands that causes the body to respond to stressful situations.

esophagus – muscular passageway connecting the mouth and oral cavity to the stomach.

estrogen – primary ovarian hormone produced by the follicle that stimulates the development and maintenance of the female reproductive system and secondary sexual characteristics.

excretion – process of eliminating metabolic waste products produced through cellular metabolism from the body.

exocrine – referring to tissues not associated with the endocrine system; usually non-hormone producing glands or organs that are in proximity to endocrine tissues.

exoskeleton – hard outer skeleton covering the body of an animal, such as the cuticle of arthropods or the shell of molluscs.

extensor – any muscle that extends a limb or joint through contraction.

eyes – external sensory receptors that receive light rays and convert them into neural impulses which are sent to the brain and interpreted as vision.

facet – a smooth, flat or rounded surface of a bone for articulation.

facial nerve – (Cranial Nerve VII) sensory/motor nerve that originates from the medulla oblongata and innervates the facial and digastric muscles, the taste buds and salivary glands.

fascia – thin sheet or band of fibrous connective tissue that binds tissues or organs together and holds them in place.

feces – excrement produced by the digestive process that is eliminated through the anus.

fimbriae – small, finger-like projections of the oviduct, the movements of which create a current which sweeps the egg into the oviduct and along its length.

flexor – any muscle that draws a limb or joint closer to the axis of the body.

follicle – a structure within the ovary that contains the developing oocyte.

follicle-stimulating hormone – pituitary hormone that stimulates sperm and ova production.

foramen – a hole to allow passage of blood vessels or nerves.

fossa – a broad, shallow, depressed area.

fovea – focal point of the eye; region of the retina where a dense conglomeration of cones exists.

frontal – situated toward the ventral half of the body; denoting a longitudinal plane.

gallbladder – organ located on the underside of the liver which stores bile and releases it into the duodenum.

gamete – reproductive cell produced in the gonads through meiosis; a haploid egg or sperm cell.

gestation – the period of embryonic development from the time of fertilization to birth in viviparous (live-bearing) species.

glans penis – the expanded distal end of the penis.

glomerulus – capillary bed of the nephron that filters out fluids and small chemical particles from the blood into the surrounding Bowmanís capsule.

glossopharyngeal nerve – (Cranial Nerve IX) sensory/motor nerve that innervates the pharyngeal muscles and posterior one-third of the tongue.

glottis – opening in the oral cavity that leads from the nasopharynx to the larynx and trachea.

glucagon – pancreatic hormone that raises blood glucose levels.

glycogen – converted form of glucose that is stored in the liver and muscles of animals.

growth hormone – pituitary hormone which stimulates growth and metabolic functions.

gyrencephalic – convoluted surface demarcated by gyri and sulci (typically referring to the brain).

gyrus – a ridge, typically convoluted, between two cerebral grooves.

hallux – first (or innermost) digit of the hindfoot; homologous to the big toe in humans.

harderian glands – glands present near the eyes of many mammals which secrete lubricating fluids for the eyeballs.

hard palate – bony plate separating the rostral portion of the oral cavity from the nasopharynx in mammals.

head – region of the body in mammals consisting of the skull, brain and major sense organs.

hepatic portal system – system of blood vessels that carries blood from the capillary beds of the stomach, small intestines and spleen to another capillary bed in the liver, where blood is detoxified and nutrients are stored and released at a controlled rate.

hepatic portal vein – large vessel that carries nutrient-rich and toxin-laden blood from the small intestines and pancreas to the liver for detoxification and regulation of nutrient release before the blood passes to the rest of the body.

homologous structures – structures in different species that are similar due to common ancestry shared by the species.

hormone – chemical compound produced by endocrine tissue and distributed through the body via the circulatory system that communicates with target organs and tissues to produce a wide array of behavioral and physiological responses, depending on the specific hormone released.

hydrochloric acid – one of the major constituent chemicals released by the stomach as a digestive compound.

hypoglossal nerve – (Cranial Nerve XII) sensory/motor nerve that innervates muscles of the throat and tongue.

hypothalamus – region of the brain responsible for coordinating the efforts and integration of the endocrine and nervous systems; produces a wide range of hormones.

ileum – distal portion of the small intestine extending from the jejunum to the cecum; primarily responsible for absorption of nutrients.

ilium – broad, flat, uppermost region of the pelvis; it is fused with the ischium and pubis to form the pelvis.

infraorbital glands – small salivary glands which drain into the mouth and secrete digestive enzymes which aid in the breakdown of starches.

infundibulum – small stalk of nervous tissue that supports the pituitary gland.

ingestion – the process of taking in food through the oral cavity.

inguinal canal – opening in the abdominal wall through which the spermatic cord passes.

insertion – the distal point of attachment of a muscle, usually to the bone moved by that muscle.

insulin – hormone secreted by the endocrine cells of the pancreas (islets of Langerhans) that is responsible for lowering blood glucose levels by stimulating the liver to store more glucose as glycogen.

interstitial cells – hormone-producing cells situated between the seminiferous tubules of the testes that produce testosterone.

iris – region of the eye that regulates the amount of light that enters the eye and reaches the retina by contraction of the sphincter muscles of the iris.

jejunum – middle portion of the small intestine extending from the duodenum to the ileum; primarily responsible for nutrient absorption.

kidney – excretory unit located in the lumbar region of mammals; this structure filters the blood creating a highly-concentrated metabolic by-product (urine) which is sent to the urinary bladder; also responsible for maintaining a homeostatic balance of salts, fluids and ions within the body (osmoregulation).

lacrimal gland – facial gland in mammals located alongside the eye that secretes a lubricating liquid for the eye (tears).

larynx – enlarged, oval-shaped region cranial to the trachea that contains the vocal cords.

lateral – situated farther away from the midline (median plane) of the body.

lens – biconvex structure in the vertebrate eye located behind the iris; functions to focus images on the retina.

lissencephalic – a smooth, featureless surface (typically referring to the brain).

liver – large, multilobed organ of the abdominal cavity located just caudal to the diaphragm; secretes bile, filters toxins and nutrients from the blood and stores sugars.

longitudinal fissure – crevice running down the median plane of the cerebrum separating the brain into left and right hemispheres.

loop of Henle – long projection of the tubules of the nephron that descends into the medulla of the kidney; creates a concentration gradient that allows salts and water to be reabsorbed by the body while nitrogenous wastes are retained in the nephron and concentrated.

lumbar – pertaining to the lower back region of the body.

lumbosacral plexus – complex network in the pelvic region formed by the confluence of the 4th, 5th and 6th lumbar nerves and the 1st and 2nd sacral nerves.

luteinizing hormone – pituitary hormone that stimulates the testes and ovaries.

mammal – class of vertebrates characterized by animals that bear live young (typically), provide milk for their young from mammary glands, possess fur or hair and have a single lower jaw bone (the mandible).

mammary glands – modified tissues on the ventral surface of mammals that secrete milk to nourish their young.

medial – situated toward the midline of the body.

median plane – longitudinal section running down the exact midline of a bilaterally symmetrical animal.

medulla – middle region of the kidney; contains loops of Henle and some collecting ducts.

medulla oblongata – most caudal region of the vertebrate brain; controls autonomic functions such as breathing, heart rate, digestion and swallowing.

meiosis – process of cell division whereby a diploid cell undergoes reduction division and results in four haploid daughter cells, typically referred to as gametes.

melatonin – pituitary hormone which influences sexual maturation and controls body's responses to seasonal changes in day length.

mesentery – connective membrane that suspends body organs in the abdominal cavity and holds them together.

mitral valve – (also called bicuspid valve); valve of the mammalian heart that directs blood flow from the left atrium to the left ventricle.

muscle – a type of tissue specialized for creating movement through contractions of the individual fibers that make up the tissue; designed either to move an animal through its environment or to move substances through the animal.

nares – the external openings of the nasal passageway; utilized in respiration.

nasopharynx – region of the nasal passageway above the soft palate.

nephron – functional unit of the kidney; specialized subunit that filters blood and concentrates urine.

norepinephrine – adrenal hormone that mediates an animal's responses to stressful situations.

occipital region – (also called occipital lobe); posterior portion of the cerebrum where the optic lobes are located.

oculomotor nerve – (Cranial Nerve III) nerve fiber with both sensory and motor functions that leaves the brain just caudal to the optic chiasma and innervates the muscles of the eye.

olfactory bulbs – forebrain structures that receive input from chemosensory cells of the nasal epithelium.

olfactory nerves (syn.: olfactory tracts) – (Cranial Nerve I) sensory nerves emanating from the olfactory bulbs and leading to the olfactory region of the brain.

oocyte – (also called ovum); an immature egg produced in the ovary.

optic chiasma – the junction at which parts of the optic nerves cross to opposite sides of the brain.

optic disk – region of the vertebrate eye where the neurons of the optic nerve pass through the choroid layer and retina; commonly referred to as the 'blind spot' since there are no visual receptors in this area.

optic nerve – (Cranial Nerve II) large confluence of sensory nerve fibers from the photoreceptors of the eye which exits the rear of the eyeball and crosses the other optic nerve at the optic chiasma before entering the brain.

ora serrata – junction between the margin of the ciliary bodies and the anterior portion of the retina; jagged in appearance.

origin – the less movable anchor point of a muscle attachment.

os penis – (syn: bacculum) bone found in the penis of many mammals which facilitates maintaining erection.

ovarian ligaments – small ligaments that attach the caudal margins of the ovaries to the uterine horns and maintain their position in the abdominal cavity.

ovary – reproductive organ in females that produces eggs and hormones.

oviduct – tube through which the egg, upon leaving the ovary, is carried on its way to the uterine horns.

ovulation – process by which mature eggs are released from the ovaries; characterized by a surge in hormone levels and a corresponding thickening of the uterine lining.

oxytocin – posterior pituitary hormone that stimulates contractions of the uterus and mammary gland cells.

pancreas – granular organ located along the left margin of the duodenum and the caudal margin of the stomach; produces digestive enzymes and a variety of hormones.

pancreatic duct – canal through which digestive enzymes produced by the pancreas are transported to the duodenum.

parietal region – lobe of the cerebrum located on either side of the head near the base of the skull.

parotid duct – small canal leading from the parotid gland to the oral cavity through which the parotid gland releases its salivary enzymes into the mouth.

parotid gland – rather large salivary gland located near the ear of the mink.

penis – external reproductive organ of the male; deposits semen in the reproductive tract of the female and carries excretory wastes in the form of urine out of the body through the urethra.

pepsinogen – gastrointestinal compound secreted by the gastric cells of the stomach that is instrumental in the chemical digestion of food particles.

pericardial membrane – thin tissue surrounding and protecting the heart.

peripheral nervous system – compilation of sensory and motor neurons and nerve fibers associated with the forelimbs and hindlimbs of the body.

peristalsis – rhythmic contractions of the alimentary canal which propel food along its length.

pineal body – small protuberance of the cerebrum which secretes hormones into the bloodstream.

pituitary gland – endocrine gland located at the base of the hypothalamus which directs the functions of many other endocrine glands throughout the body.

plantigrade – type of locomotion characterized by walking on the soles of the feet; body weight is supported primarily by the tarsals.

pollex – first digit of the forelimb; thumb.

pons – a hindbrain structure, ventral to the medulla oblongata.

prepuce – the pocket of skin that encloses the glans penis.

process – a broad designation for any bone protrusion; usually the site of muscle or tendon attachment.

progesterone – hormone produced by the corpus luteum of the ovary that is responsible for preparing the uterus for reception and development of the fertilized eggs.

prolactin – pituitary hormone that stimulates milk production and secretion.

pronate – rotation of the hand or foot inward (the hand would rotate such that the thumb moved closer to the body; the foot would rotate such that the inner margin of the foot would strike the ground first).

prostate gland – in minks, a large, whitish gland located at the junction of the vas deferentia and the urethra; produces accessory seminal fluids.

proximal – situated toward the trunk of the body, closer to the median plane (e.g., your elbow is proximal to your hand).

pulmonary arteries – short blood vessels which, in the adult, carry deoxygenated blood from the right ventricle of the heart to the lungs.

pulmonary veins – blood vessels which, in the adult, carry oxygenated blood from the lungs to the left atrium of the heart.

pupil – opening in the iris of the eye; its size is controlled by contractions of the sphincter muscles of the iris to regulate the amount of light that enters the eye.

quadrupedal – describes an animal that walks on all four legs.

rectum – distal end of the intestinal tract; primary function is to reabsorb water and produce dry, concentrated feces.

renal pelvis – innermost region of the kidney; contains the collecting ducts and the origin of the ureter.

retina – specialized layer of the vertebrate eye that contains the photoreceptive cells (the rods and cones).

rod – type of photoreceptor that ìseesî images as only black and white; these cells are very good at detecting motion and contribute to extremely high visual acuity.

rostral – situated toward the tip of the nose.

rugae – ridges and folds of the inner wall of the stomach which increase the surface area of the stomach lining and provide texture for the manipulation of food as it is broken down.

sacral – pertaining to the sacrum.

sacrum – wedge-shaped portion of the pelvis that is formed by the fusion of vertebrae and serves to support the pelvic girdle and hindlimbs.

sagittal – refers to a plane running the length of the body parallel to the median plane.

sagittal fissure – crevice running down the median plane of the cerebrum separating the brain into left and right hemispheres.

saliva – liquid secretion of the salivary glands that lubricates food to facilitate swallowing and contains enzymes which initiate the digestive process.

salivary glands – special glands located within the oral cavity and neck that produce a variety of fluids and enzymes that facilitate digestion.

sclera – tough, outer covering of the eye; gives the outer eyeball its white coloration; protects the delicate inner structures and serves as a tissue for muscle attachments.

scrotal sacs – pouches extending from the caudal region of the mink which contain the testes (after they have descended from the abdominal cavity during embryonic development). Their presence allows the temperature of the testes to be maintained at a slighter lower temperature than that of the abdominal cavity.

secondary palate – region that constitutes the ìroof of the mouth,î separating the nasal passageway from the oral cavity; in mammals it is comprised of the hard and soft palates.

semen – mixture containing sperm cells and accessory fluids secreted by the reproductive glands of the male; serves to provide a nutrient base for the sperm as well as keep them moist and neutralize the acidity of the vagina to increase sperm survival.

semilunar valve – flaps of tissue at the junction of each ventricle of the heart to prevent backflow of blood from either the pulmonary arteries or aorta into their respective ventricles.

seminal vesicles – accessory glands of the male reproductive system located near the junction of the urethra and base of the penis; they contribute fluid to the semen that contains nutrients for the sperm and stimulates uterine contractions to assist in directing the sperm toward the egg.

seminiferous tubules – tubule system located inside the testes where sperm are produced through meiosis. Primary spermatocytes are formed along the outer margins of the seminiferous tubules and migrate inward as they mature.

sensory neuron – specialized nerve cell that is capable of receiving external stimuli and sending a nerve impulse through the nervous system to the spinal cord and brain.

skeletal muscle – type of muscle tissue characterized by striated fibers and multinucleated cells; typically under voluntary control.

skull – hard, bony, protective covering of the brain.

smooth muscle – type of muscle tissue characterized by fibers with no striations and a single nucleus in each muscle cell; typically involuntary.

soft palate – cartilaginous region of the roof of the mouth that separates the oral cavity from the nasal passageway; located toward the back of the mouth.

somatostatin – pancreatic hormone that regulates the levels of insulin and glucagon in the blood.

spermatic cord – long, narrow tube that leads from the testis through the abdominal wall and contains the vas deferens, the spermatic artery and vein, lymphatic vessels and numerous nerves.

spinal cord – thin extension of the central nervous system that runs along the length of the body, protected by the bony vertebrae.

spleen – ductless, vascular organ in the abdominal cavity that is a component of the circulatory system; stores blood, recycles worn-out red blood cells and produces lymphocytes.

stomach – large U-shaped digestive reservoir for food. In addition to storing large quantities of food, chemicals are secreted by the walls of the stomach which break down the food into microscopic particles that may be absorbed by the cells of the intestines.

sublingual gland – salivary gland located underneath the skin and alongside the tongue of the mink.

submaxillary gland – oval-shaped salivary gland located underneath the large parotid gland.

sulcus – a furrow or groove (often referring to features of the brain).

superficial – lying near the surface.

supinate – rotation of the hand or foot outward (the hand would rotate such that the thumb moved away from the body; the foot would rotate such that the outer margin of the foot would strike the ground first).

suspensory ovarian ligaments – short ligaments that attach the cranial margins of the ovaries to the dorsal body wall and maintain their position in the abdominal cavity.

synarthrosis – a joint in which there is little or no movement (e.g., sutures found between the bones of the skull or of the sacrum).

tactile – relating to or pertaining to the sense of touch.

tapetum lucidum – reflective coating of the choroid layer of the eye of some mammals which increases their ability to see at night and is responsible for the phenomenon of ìeye shine.î

tendon – fibrous cord of connective tissue which typically serves as an attachment between muscle and bone.

testis – reproductive organ of the male which produces sperm and hormones.

testosterone – the principal male sex hormone; responsible for the development and maintenance of male secondary sexual characteristics and sex drive.

thoracic – pertaining to the chest region.

thorax – region of the body from the base of the neck to the plane where the diaphragm extends across the body cavity.

thymosin – hormone produced by the thymus gland which stimulates the action of the immune system.

thymus – endocrine gland located along the lateral margins of the trachea near the larynx and lying on the cranial margin of the pericardial membrane surrounding the heart; produces thymosin.

thyroid – oval-shaped endocrine gland located on the ventral surface of the trachea just caudal to the larynx; produces thyroxine and calcitonin.

thyroid-stimulating hormone – pituitary hormone that stimulates the thyroid gland.

thyroxine – thyroid hormone responsible for controlling metabolic and growth rates.

tongue – muscular structure located in the oral cavity and used for manipulation of food.

trachea – cartilaginous tube extending from the larynx to the lungs through which air is transported during respiration.

transverse – referring to a plane separating the body into cranial and caudal portions (perpendicular to the median plane).

tricuspid valve – flaps of tissue at the junction of the right atrium and right ventricle which prevent backflow of blood into the right atrium.

trigeminal nerve – (Cranial Nerve V) sensory/motor nerve which emanates from the posterior portion of the pons and consists of the ophthalmic, maxillary and mandibular branches.

trochlear nerves – (Cranial Nerve IV) extremely small nerves with both sensory and motor functions that innervate eye muscles.

trunk – region of the body extending from the plane where the diaphragm bisects the body to the base of the tail.

tubercle – a small, rounded bony eminence.

tuberosity – a large, rounded bony eminence.

ureter – tube that transports urine from the kidney to the urinary bladder for storage.

urethra – tube that leads from the urinary bladder to the outside of the body; transports urine and (in males) semen.

urinary bladder – membranous sac that serves as a receptacle for excreted urine from the kidneys.

urine – fluid excreted by the kidneys, stored in the urinary bladder and eliminated from the body through the urethra; composed primarily of nitrogenous wastes and excess salts and sugars.

urogenital sinus – common chamber for reproductive and excretory products in the female; located just caudal to the junction of the vagina and urethra.

uterus – region where embryonic development of the fetus occurs; in minks the uterus is divided into the body of the uterus and two uterine horns. The uterine horns are where fetal development occurs in the mink.

vagina – female reproductive canal leading from the cervix to the urogenital sinus.

vagus nerve – (Cranial Nerve X) sensory/motor nerve that innervates the pharynx, larynx, heart, lungs, diaphragm and abdominal organs.

vas deferens – tube connected to the epididymis that transports sperm from the testis through the epididymis to the urethra during ejaculation.

vein – blood vessel that carries blood toward the heart.

ventral – situated toward the belly region of an animal.

ventricle – large muscular chamber of the heart that pumps blood out of the heart into an artery.

vermis – narrow median portion of the cerebellum separating the two cerebellar hemispheres.

vertebrate – animal that possesses bony vertebrae that surround the spinal cord.

vestibule – common chamber for reproductive and excretory products in the female; located just caudal to the junction of the vagina and urethra.

vibrissae – hairs that project outward from the head of an animal and respond to tactile stimuli (often called whiskers).

vitreous chamber – posterior fluid-filled chamber of the eye that contains the lens.

vitreous humor – clear, jelly-like liquid that fills the vitreous chamber; provides support and cushioning for the lens and internal structures of the eye.

vulva – most caudal region of the female urogenital tract consisting of the vestibule, clitoris and labia.

Index